Chicago Writer **Books**

A Guide to

Children's

Book

Publishers

What They Publish, Who They Hire, and How to Get Connected

- ✓ Up-to-date i̶n̶_____ ̶_____ ̶s̶ialializing in children's ti̶_____ ̶enting
- ✓ Listed alpha̶_____ te links
- ✓ New inform̶_____ tance, internships̶_____
- ✓ Represent̶_____ what you're writ̶___

Acknowledgements

iWrite Publications Inc. gratefully acknowledges all of the publishers who took the time to verify their information and complete our questionnaire. It is their efforts that make this guide valuable to the writers, editors, and associated freelancers who wish to do business with them.

Published by:
iWrite Publications Inc.
P.O. Box 10923, Chicago, IL 60610-0923
iwriteinc@aol.com

Disclaimer

Chicago Writer

Keep up-to-date with issues that affect writers, editors, and publishing professionals.
Visit our web site at http://www.ChicagoWriter.com.

Introduction

This guide is a compilation of the children's book publishers in the US. The companies are listed alphabetically, by name.

Note: You may notice some irregularity in the alphabetization of the publishers' names, especially those imprints named after people. Some are alphabetized by first name, some last name. We are honoring the publishers' preferences and including them in our listing as they would, e.g., Wendy Lamb Books can be found under "L," William Morrow under "W."

Using the Guide

The intent of this guide is to provide you—the prospective employee, author, or freelancer—advance intelligence about your market. Use this guide to target your skills and interests to a publisher's scope and needs.

There are over 160 publishers listed in this guide. Most of them purchase manuscripts and hire on a regular basis—particular skill sets for their particular needs.

Use this guide to research the publishers. With an Internet connection and web link information, you can connect to the company's web site with ease. The publishers' sites provide more in-depth profiles of the companies, as well as information such as: job opportunities, writer's guidelines, current publishing lists, and additional contact and business information.

Manuscript Submissions

When approaching a publisher to sell a manuscript, do your homework and be respectful of their processes.

- Become familiar with the types of books in which the publisher specializes. Websites provide an abundance of information.
- Read and follow their submission guidelines. If guidelines are not published on the website, it's acceptable to call and ask how they may be obtained.
- Prepare your manuscript as instructed and make sure it's your best effort.
- Include a short cover letter briefly outlining the concept of your book, the age range of the audience, and a synopsis of your writing/publishing credentials, if applicable.
- As a courtesy, include a self-addressed, stamped envelope (SASE) in the package for the editor's response.

Corrections/Updates

As diligent as we might be, businesses change—companies merge, people move jobs, and publishing priorities change. If you find any information that is out-of-date or publishers that you think should be added or removed from the guide, please drop us an email at iwriteinc@aol.com to let us know. We appreciate your assistance.

Good luck in your publishing quests!

Table of Contents

Abbeville Kids

An Imprint of Abbeville Press
116 West 23rd Street, New York, NY 10011
(646) 375 2038

Established:	–	# of Employees:	–
Titles in Print:	–	Published Annually:	–

What They Publish

Publishes books for children of all ages.

Representative Titles/Projects

- *Women of Camelot*
- *Big League Dreams*
- *Holes: Silly Shapes*

Who They Hire

Authors/Writers:

Pays royalties/advances. Buys all rights.

Editors, proofreaders, illustrators, designers, production personnel:

Rates vary. Send cover letter with current résumé.

Internships/Summer Jobs:

Internships available: ☐ Yes ☒ No   Summer Jobs Available: ☐ Yes ☒ No

How to Get Connected

Contact:

Robert Abrams, Editorial Director

Accepts unsolicited/unagented manuscripts: ☒ Yes ☐ No
Accepts queries by: ☐ Email ☐ Fax ☐ Phone ☒ Letter
Query first. Responds if interested.

✉ Email:
🌐 Web Site: http://www.abbeville.com

Abrams Books for Young Readers

115 West 18th Street, New York, NY 10011
(212) 519 1200

Established:	1987	# of Employees:	–
Titles in Print:	150	Published Annually:	40–50

What They Publish

Publishes fiction and picture books for children.

Representative Titles/Projects

- *Animalia*
- *Babar and the Succotash Bird*
- *Hello Kitty®, Hello World*

Who They Hire

Authors/Writers:
Pays royalties/advances. Buys all rights.

Editors, proofreaders, illustrators, designers, production personnel:
Rates vary. Send cover letter with current résumé.

Internships/Summer Jobs:
Internships available: ☐ Yes ☒ No   Summer Jobs Available: ☐ Yes ☒ No

How to Get Connected

Contact:
Howard Reeves, Vice President, Gift and Children's Books

Accepts unsolicited/unagented manuscripts: ☒ Yes ☐ No
Accepts queries by: ☐ Email ☐ Fax ☐ Phone ☒ Letter
Query first. Responds if interested.

✉ Email:
🌐 Web Site: http://www.abramsbooks.com

Academy Chicago Publishers

363 W. Erie Street, Chicago, IL 60610
(312) 751 7300

Established:	1975	# of Employees:	6
Titles in Print:	365	Published Annually:	varies

What They Publish

Publishes fiction, nonfiction, and out-of-print works of the classics (on case-by-case basis). Focuses on mysteries, history, and biography for the adult market.

Currently accepting new manuscripts on all topics.

Representative Titles/Projects

- *Sharon: Israel's Warrior – Politician*, by Anita Miller, Jordan Miller, and Sigalit Zetouni
- *Letters in the Attic*, by Bonnie Shimko
- *A Fly Has a Hundred Eyes*, by Aileen Baron

Who They Hire

Writers:
Pays royalties, rates vary/may pay advances. Buys all rights.

Publicity, production:
Currently not hiring full time positions. Send cover letter with current résumé.

Artists:
Uses freelance artists on occasion. Send cover letter with current résumé.

Internships/Summer Jobs:
Internships available: ☐ Yes ☒ No   Summer Jobs Available: ☐ Yes ☒ No

How to Get Connected

Contact:
Dr. Anita Miller, President and Editor
Jordan Miller, Vice President

Accepts unsolicited/unagented manuscripts: ☒ Yes ☐ No
Accepts queries by: ☐ Email ☐ Fax ☐ Phone ☒ Letter
Replies within two months.

✉ Email: academy363@aol.com
🌐 Web Site: http://www.academychicago.com

Accord Publishing Ltd.

1732 Wazee Street, Suite 202, Denver, CO 80202
(888) 333 1676

Established:	–	# of Employees:	–
Titles in Print:	–	Published Annually:	–

What They Publish

Publishes children's books, puppets, and educational science kits.

Representative Titles/Projects

- *Barnyard Boogie*
- *Frog in the Kitchen Sink*
- *Firsts: Reflections of a 7-Year-Old*

Who They Hire

Authors/Writers:
Pays royalties/advances. Buys all rights.

Editors, proofreaders, illustrators, designers, production personnel:
Rates vary. Send cover letter with current résumé.

Internships/Summer Jobs:
Internships available: ☐ Yes ☒ No   Summer Jobs Available: ☐ Yes ☒ No

How to Get Connected

Contact:
Ken Fleck, President

Accepts unsolicited/unagented manuscripts: ☒ Yes   ☐ No
Accepts queries by: ☐ Email ☐ Fax ☐ Phone ☒ Letter
Query first. Responds if interested.

✉ Email:
🌐 Web Site: http://www.accordpublishing.com

Action Publishing

PO Box 391, Glendale, CA 91209
(800) 644 2665

Established:	1996	# of Employees:	–
Titles in Print:	–	Published Annually:	–

What They Publish

Publishes children's books.

Representative Titles/Projects

- *Look at the Size of That Long-Legged Ploot*
- *The Monster of Manners*
- *Legend of Snow Pookas*

Who They Hire

Authors/Writers:
Pays royalties/advances. Buys all rights.

Editors, proofreaders, illustrators, designers, production personnel:
Rates vary. Send cover letter with current résumé.

Internships/Summer Jobs:
Internships available: ☐ Yes ☒ No   Summer Jobs Available: ☐ Yes ☒ No

How to Get Connected

Contact:
Michael Metzler, Publisher

Accepts unsolicited/unagented manuscripts: ☒ Yes ☐ No
Accepts queries by: ☐ Email ☐ Fax ☐ Phone ☒ Letter
Query first. Responds if interested.

✉ Email: publisher@actionpublishing.com
🌐 Web Site: http://www.actionpublishing.com

Active Parenting Publishers

1955 Vaughn Road, #108, Kennesaw, GA 30144-7808
(770) 429 0565

Established:	1980	# of Employees:	–
Titles in Print:	–	Published Annually:	–

What They Publish

Publishes books on parenting, self-help, and counseling.

Representative Titles/Projects

- The Heart of Parenting Series
- The School Success Series
- *Active Parenting Now*

Who They Hire

Authors/Writers:
Pays royalties/advances. Buys all rights.

Editors, proofreaders, illustrators, designers, production personnel:
Rates vary. Send cover letter with current résumé.

Internships/Summer Jobs:
Internships available: ☐ Yes ☒ No   Summer Jobs Available: ☐ Yes ☒ No

How to Get Connected

Contact:
Michael Popkin, President

Accepts unsolicited/unagented manuscripts: ☒ Yes   ☐ No
Accepts queries by: ☐ Email ☐ Fax ☐ Phone ☒ Letter
Query first. Responds if interested.

✉ Email: mpopkin@activeparenting.com
🌐 Web Site: http://www.activeparenting.com

African American Images

1909 W. 95th Street, Chicago, Illinois 60643
(773) 445 0322

Established:	1983	# of Employees:	10
Titles in Print:	80	Published Annually:	6

What They Publish

Publishes Africentric books on self-esteem, collective values, liberation, and skill development topics for children and adults.

Representative Titles/Projects

- *Black Students/Middle Class Teachers*
- *Race Code War*
- *Grandma's Ashanti Cloth*

Who They Hire

Writers:
Pays royalties/advances.

Editors, proofreaders, illustrators, designers, indexers, production personnel:
Rates vary. Send cover letter with current résumé.

Internships/Summer Jobs:
Internships available: ☐ Yes ☒ No   Summer Jobs Available: ☐ Yes ☒ No

How to Get Connected

Contact:
Jawanza Kunjufu, President

Accepts unsolicited/unagented manuscripts: ☒ Yes ☐ No
Accepts queries by: ☐ Email ☐ Fax ☐ Phone ☒ Letter
Query first. Responds in 8–10 weeks.

✉ Email: aai@africanamericanimages.com
🌐 Web Site: http://africanamericanimages.com

Alef Design Group

4423 Fruitland Avenue, Los Angeles, CA 90058

Established:	–	# of Employees:	–
Titles in Print:	–	Published Annually:	–

What They Publish

Publishes young adult novels and children's books for Jewish children.

Representative Titles/Projects

- *God's Paintbrush*
- *Rafi's Search*
- *Sense of Shabbat*

Who They Hire

Authors/Writers:
Pays royalties/advances. Buys all rights.

Editors, proofreaders, illustrators, designers, production personnel:
Rates vary. Send cover letter with current résumé.

Internships/Summer Jobs:
Internships available: ☐ Yes ☒ No   Summer Jobs Available: ☐ Yes ☒ No

How to Get Connected

Contact:
Jane Golub, Editor

Accepts unsolicited/unagented manuscripts: ☒ Yes ☐ No
Accepts queries by: ☐ Email ☐ Fax ☐ Phone ☒ Letter
Query first. Responds if interested.

✉ Email: misrad@torahaura.com
🌐 Web Site: http://www.alefdesign.com or http://www.torahaura.com

All About Kids Publishing

6280 San Ignacio Avenue, #C, San Jose, CA 95119
(408) 578 4026

Established:	–	# of Employees:	–
Titles in Print:	–	Published Annually:	–

What They Publish

Publishes children's picture books.

Representative Titles/Projects

-
-
-

Who They Hire

Authors/Writers:
Pays royalties/advances. Buys all rights.

Editors, proofreaders, illustrators, designers, production personnel:
Rates vary. Send cover letter with current résumé.

Internships/Summer Jobs:
Internships available: ☐ Yes ☒ No   Summer Jobs Available: ☐ Yes ☒ No

How to Get Connected

Contact:
Editor

Accepts unsolicited/unagented manuscripts: ☒ Yes ☐ No
Accepts queries by: ☐ Email ☐ Fax ☐ Phone ☒ Letter
Query first. Responds if interested.

✉ Email:
🌐 Web Site:

Amadeus Press

512 Newark Pompton Turnpike, Pompton Plains, NJ 07444
(414) 774 3630

Established:	1987	# of Employees:	–
Titles in Print:	–	Published Annually:	–

What They Publish

Publishes children's books about music.

Representative Titles/Projects

- *Polly and the Piano*
-
-

Who They Hire

Authors/Writers:
Pays royalties/advances. Buys all rights.

Editors, proofreaders, illustrators, designers, production personnel:
Rates vary. Send cover letter with current résumé.

Internships/Summer Jobs:
Internships available: ☐ Yes ☒ No   Summer Jobs Available: ☐ Yes ☒ No

How to Get Connected

Contact:
John Cerullo, Publisher

Accepts unsolicited/unagented manuscripts: ☒ Yes ☐ No
Accepts queries by: ☐ Email ☐ Fax ☐ Phone ☒ Letter
Query first. Responds if interested.

✉ Email:
🌐 Web Site: http://www.amadeuspress.com

Atheneum Books for Young Readers

1230 Avenue of the Americas, New York, NY 10020

Established:	–	# of Employees:	–
Titles in Print:	–	Published Annually:	–

What They Publish

Publishes children's books.

Representative Titles/Projects

- *Birthday Bugs*
- Eloise Series
- Nancy Drew Girl Detective Series

Who They Hire

Authors/Writers:
Pays royalties/advances. Buys all rights.

Editors, proofreaders, illustrators, designers, production personnel:
Rates vary. Send cover letter with current résumé.

Internships/Summer Jobs:
Internships available: ☒ Yes ☐ No   Summer Jobs Available: ☐ Yes ☒ No

How to Get Connected

Contact:
Ginee Seo, Editor

Accepts unsolicited/unagented manuscripts: ☐ Yes ☒ No
Accepts queries by: ☐ Email ☐ Fax ☐ Phone ☒ Letter
Query only. Responds if interested.

✉ Email:
🌐 Web Site: http://www.simonsayskids.com

Augsburg Books

Augsburg Fortress Publishers
PO Box 1209, Minneapolis, MN 55440
(612) 330 3300

Established:	–	# of Employees:	–
Titles in Print:	–	Published Annually:	–

What They Publish

Publishes religious books for children.

Representative Titles/Projects

- *A Friend from Galilee*
- *Papa's Birthday Gift*
- *You Are So Wonderful*

Who They Hire

Authors/Writers:
Pays royalties/advances. Buys all rights.

Editors, proofreaders, illustrators, designers, production personnel:
Rates vary. Send cover letter with current résumé.

Internships/Summer Jobs:
Internships available: ☐ Yes ☒ No   Summer Jobs Available: ☐ Yes ☒ No

How to Get Connected

Contact:
Editor

Accepts unsolicited/unagented manuscripts: ☒ Yes   ☐ No
Accepts queries by: ☐ Email ☐ Fax ☐ Phone ☒ Letter
Submission guidelines on website.

✉ Email:
🌐 Web Site: http://www.augsburgbooks.com

August House Publishers

PO Box 3223, Little Rock, AR 72203
(501) 372 5450

Established:	1979	# of Employees:	–
Titles in Print:	250	Published Annually:	–

What They Publish

Publishes folk tale anthologies, storytelling guides, and illustrated books.

Representative Titles/Projects

- *It Rained All Day That Night*
- *East African Folktales*
- *Boy Who Loved Frogs*

Who They Hire

Authors/Writers:
Pays royalties/advances. Buys all rights.

Editors, proofreaders, illustrators, designers, production personnel:
Rates vary. Send cover letter with current résumé.

Internships/Summer Jobs:
Internships available: ☐ Yes ☒ No   Summer Jobs Available: ☐ Yes ☒ No

How to Get Connected

Contact:
Liz Parkhurst, CEO

Accepts unsolicited/unagented manuscripts: ☒ Yes ☐ No
Accepts queries by: ☐ Email ☐ Fax ☐ Phone ☒ Letter
Query first. Responds if interested.

✉ Email: es_parkhurst@augusthouse.com
🌐 Web Site: http://www.augusthouse.com

Barefoot Books

3 Bow Street, Cambridge, MA 02138
(617) 576 0660

Established:	1993	# of Employees:	23
Titles in Print:	–	Published Annually:	–

What They Publish

Publishes books that celebrate art and story and inspire children to explore their own creative gifts.

Representative Titles/Projects

- *Animal Boogie*
- *Celtic Memories*
- *Gigantic Turnip*

Who They Hire

Authors/Writers:
Pays royalties/advances. Buys all rights.

Editors, proofreaders, illustrators, designers, production personnel:
Rates vary. Send cover letter with current résumé.

Internships/Summer Jobs:
Internships available: ☐ Yes ☒ No   Summer Jobs Available: ☐ Yes ☒ No

How to Get Connected

Contact:
Tessa Strickland, Nancy Traversy, Publishers

Accepts unsolicited/unagented manuscripts: ☒ Yes ☐ No
Accepts queries by: ☐ Email ☐ Fax ☐ Phone ☒ Letter
Query first. Responds if interested.

✉ Email:
🌐 Web Site: http://www.barefootbooks.com

Barron's Educational Series

250 Wireless Boulevard, Hauppauge, NY 11788

Established:	1941	# of Employees:	–
Titles in Print:	2,000	Published Annually:	–

What They Publish

Publishes children's books.

Representative Titles/Projects

- *There Is a Little Prince in Every Frog*
- *Zoo Poo*
- *Cooking Outside the Pizza Box*

Who They Hire

Authors/Writers:
Pays royalties/advances. Buys all rights.

Editors, proofreaders, illustrators, designers, production personnel:
Rates vary. Send cover letter with current résumé.

Internships/Summer Jobs:
Internships available: ☒ Yes ☐ No   Summer Jobs Available: ☐ Yes ☒ No

How to Get Connected

Contact:
Editor

Accepts unsolicited/unagented manuscripts: ☒ Yes   ☐ No
Accepts queries by: ☐ Email ☐ Fax ☐ Phone ☒ Letter
Query first. Responds if interested.

✉ Email:
🌐 Web Site: http://www.barronseduc.com

Bay Light Publishing

PO Box 3032, Mooresville, NC 28117
(866) 541 3895

Established:	–	# of Employees:	–
Titles in Print:	–	Published Annually:	–

What They Publish

Publishes books that inspire, motivate and educate children about the Bible.

Representative Titles/Projects

- *Thank You, Noah*
- *Thank You, Jesus*
- *Thank You, Peter*

Who They Hire

Authors/Writers:
Pays royalties/advances. Buys all rights.

Editors, proofreaders, illustrators, designers, production personnel:
Rates vary. Send cover letter with current résumé.

Internships/Summer Jobs:
Internships available: ☐ Yes ☒ No   Summer Jobs Available: ☐ Yes ☒ No

How to Get Connected

Contact:
Charlotte Lundy, Publisher

Accepts unsolicited/unagented manuscripts: ☒ Yes ☐ No
Accepts queries by: ☐ Email ☐ Fax ☐ Phone ☒ Letter
Query first. Responds if interested.

✉ Email: charlotte@baylightpub.com
🌐 Web Site: http://www.baylightpub.com

Bendon Publishing International

718 Clark Avenue, Ashland, OH 44805
(419) 281 5985

Established:	2001	# of Employees:	–
Titles in Print:	–	Published Annually:	–

What They Publish

Publishes a full line of storybooks, pop-up books, and activity books and merchandise for children.

Representative Titles/Projects

- Muppet Babies Series
- Garfield Series
- My Little Pony Series

Who They Hire

Authors/Writers:
Pays royalties/advances. Buys all rights.

Editors, proofreaders, illustrators, designers, production personnel:
Rates vary. Send cover letter with current résumé.

Internships/Summer Jobs:
Internships available: ☐ Yes ☒ No   Summer Jobs Available: ☐ Yes ☒ No

How to Get Connected

Contact:
 Publisher

Accepts unsolicited/unagented manuscripts: ☒ Yes   ☐ No
Accepts queries by: ☐ Email ☐ Fax ☐ Phone ☒ Letter
Query first. Responds if interested.

✉ Email:
🌐 Web Site: http://www.bendonpub.com

Beyond Words

20827 NW Cornell Road, Suite 500, Hillsboro, OR 97124
(503) 531 8700

Established:	1984	# of Employees:	–
Titles in Print:	100	Published Annually:	–

What They Publish

Publishes children's books that inspire, delight, and educate.

Representative Titles/Projects

- *Better Than a Lemonade Stand*
- *The Book of Faeries*
- *The Girl Who Hated Books*

Who They Hire

Authors/Writers:
Pays royalties/advances. Buys all rights.

Editors, proofreaders, illustrators, designers, production personnel:
Rates vary. Send cover letter with current résumé.

Internships/Summer Jobs:
Internships available: ☐ Yes ☒ No   Summer Jobs Available: ☐ Yes ☒ No

How to Get Connected

Contact:
Michelle Roehm, Children's Books Editor

Accepts unsolicited/unagented manuscripts: ☒ Yes ☐ No
Accepts queries by: ☐ Email ☐ Fax ☐ Phone ☒ Letter
Submission guidelines on website.

✉ Email: info@beyondword.com
🌐 Web Site: http://www.beyondword.com

Bloomsbury Children's

Bloomsbury USA
175 Fifth Avenue, Suite 712, New York, NY 10010

Established:	2001	# of Employees:	–
Titles in Print:	–	Published Annually:	–

What They Publish

Purchases UK rights for children's books.

Representative Titles/Projects

- *Christopher Mouse*
- *By Word of Mouse*
- *The Noisy Farm*

Who They Hire

Authors/Writers:
Pays royalties/advances. Buys all rights.

Editors, proofreaders, illustrators, designers, production personnel:
Does not hire.

Internships/Summer Jobs:
Internships available: ☐ Yes ☒ No   Summer Jobs Available: ☐ Yes ☒ No

How to Get Connected

Contact:
Sarah Odedina, Ele Fountain, Editors

Accepts unsolicited/unagented manuscripts: ☒ Yes ☐ No
Accepts queries by: ☐ Email ☐ Fax ☐ Phone ☒ Letter
Query first. Responds if interested.

✉ Email: info@bloomsburyusa.com
🌐 Web Site: http://www.bloomsburyusa.com

Blue Apple Books

515 South Valley Road, Maplewood, NJ 07040
(973) 763 8191

Established:	1987	# of Employees:	–
Titles in Print:	–	Published Annually:	–

What They Publish

Publishes high quality board, picture, and storybooks for children.

Representative Titles/Projects

- *Buzzy's Boo-Boo*
- *Does a Duck Have a Daddy?*
- *Does a Yak Get a Haircut?*

Who They Hire

Authors/Writers:
Pays royalties/advances. Buys all rights.

Editors, proofreaders, illustrators, designers, production personnel:
Rates vary. Send cover letter with current résumé.

Internships/Summer Jobs:
Internships available: ☐ Yes ☒ No   Summer Jobs Available: ☐ Yes ☒ No

How to Get Connected

Contact:
Harriet Ziefert, Publisher

Accepts unsolicited/unagented manuscripts: ☒ Yes ☐ No
Accepts queries by: ☐ Email ☐ Fax ☐ Phone ☒ Letter
Query first. Responds if interested.

✉ Email: hmziefinc@aol.com
🌐 Web Site: http://www.blueapplebooks.com

Blue Marlin Publications

823 Aberdeen Road, West Bay Shore, NY 11706
(631) 666 0353

Established:	1999	# of Employees:	–
Titles in Print:	–	Published Annually:	–

What They Publish

Publishes quality children's and young adult books that allow them to laugh as they learn.

Representative Titles/Projects

- *In the Shadow of the Moment*
- *The Teacher Who Would Not Retire*
-

Who They Hire

Authors/Writers:
Pays royalties/advances. Buys all rights.

Editors, proofreaders, illustrators, designers, production personnel:
Rates vary. Send cover letter with current résumé.

Internships/Summer Jobs:
Internships available: ☐ Yes ☒ No   Summer Jobs Available: ☐ Yes ☒ No

How to Get Connected

Contact:
Francine Poppo Rich, Publisher

Accepts unsolicited/unagented manuscripts: ☒ Yes   ☐ No
Accepts queries by: ☐ Email ☐ Fax ☐ Phone ☒ Letter
Submission guidelines on website. Responds in 8–10 weeks.

✉ Email: AbigMarlin@aol.com
🌐 Web Site: http://www.bluemarlinpubs.com

BOW Books

Blessing Our World
PO Box 185848, Fort Worth, TX 76181
(800) 729 1130

Established:	–	# of Employees:	–
Titles in Print:	–	Published Annually:	–

What They Publish

Publishes children's religious books and audio promoting character development.

Representative Titles/Projects

- *What Good Is*
- *Chris Mouse and the Christmas House*
-

Who They Hire

Authors/Writers:
Pays royalties/advances. Buys all rights.

Editors, proofreaders, illustrators, designers, production personnel:
Rates vary. Send cover letter with current résumé.

Internships/Summer Jobs:
Internships available: ☐ Yes ☒ No   Summer Jobs Available: ☐ Yes ☒ No

How to Get Connected

Contact:
Gerald Luke, Publisher

Accepts unsolicited/unagented manuscripts: ☒ Yes ☐ No
Accepts queries by: ☐ Email ☐ Fax ☐ Phone ☒ Letter
Query first. Responds if interested.

✉ Email: Gerald@bowbooks.com
🌐 Web Site: http://www.blessworld.com or http://www.bowbooks.com

Boyds Mills Press

815 Church Street, Honesdale, PA 18431
(570) 253 1164

Established:	–	# of Employees:	–
Titles in Print:	–	Published Annually:	–

What They Publish

Publishes for children from preschool to young adult.

Representative Titles/Projects

- *'Til the Cows Come Home*
- *Dog of Discovery*
- *Water Music*

Who They Hire

Authors/Writers:
Pays royalties/advances. Buys all rights.

Editors, proofreaders, illustrators, designers, production personnel:
Rates vary. Send cover letter with current résumé.

Internships/Summer Jobs:
Internships available: ☐ Yes ☒ No   Summer Jobs Available: ☐ Yes ☒ No

How to Get Connected

Contact:
Larry Rosler, Editorial Director

Accepts unsolicited/unagented manuscripts: ☒ Yes ☐ No
Accepts queries by: ☐ Email ☐ Fax ☐ Phone ☒ Letter
Query first. Responds if interested.

✉ Email:
🌐 Web Site: http://www.boydsmillspress.com

Brethren Press

Division of Church of the Brethren General Board
1451 Dundee Avenue, Elgin, IL 60120
(847) 742 5100

Established:	1897	# of Employees:	n/a
Titles in Print:	100	Published Annually:	5

What They Publish

Publishes books on Bible study, theology, church history, personal lifestyle issues, social concerns, peace and justice, devotional life, and personal growth for Christian adults and children.

Note: Authors should not query this publisher. They are not accepting material as they have scaled back their book publishing operation at this time to focus on curriculum and congregational resources.

Representative Titles/Projects

- *Through the Bible in One Year—Great Truths of the Bible*
- *Let Our Joys Be Known*
- *Children of the Bible*, by Charlotte Stowell

Who They Hire

Writers:
Pays royalties/advances. Buys all rights.

Editors, proofreaders, illustrators, designers, indexers, production personnel:
Rates vary. Send cover letter with current résumé.

Internships/Summer Jobs:
Internships available: ☒ Yes ☐ No   Summer Jobs Available: ☐ Yes ☒ No

How to Get Connected

Contact:
Wendy McFadden, Director

Accepts unsolicited/unagented manuscripts: ☐ Yes ☒ No
Accepts queries by: ☐ Email ☐ Fax ☐ Phone ☐ Letter

✉ Email: brethren_press_gb@brethren.org
🌐 Web Site: http://www.brethren.org

The Brookfield Reader

137 Peyton Road, Sterling, VA 20165
(888) 389 2741

Established:	–	# of Employees:	–
Titles in Print:	–	Published Annually:	–

What They Publish

Publishes books filled with information, thought-provoking ideas, and a sense of wonder about all life.

Representative Titles/Projects

- *The Jonathan Adventures*
- *The ABC of Artistry*
-

Who They Hire

Authors/Writers:
Pays royalties/advances. Buys all rights.

Editors, proofreaders, illustrators, designers, production personnel:
Rates vary. Send cover letter with current résumé.

Internships/Summer Jobs:
Internships available: ☐ Yes ☒ No   Summer Jobs Available: ☐ Yes ☒ No

How to Get Connected

Contact:
Susan Baggette, Publisher

Accepts unsolicited/unagented manuscripts: ☒ Yes ☐ No
Accepts queries by: ☐ Email ☐ Fax ☐ Phone ☒ Letter
Query first. Responds if interested.

✉ Email: info@brookfieldreader.com
🌐 Web Site: http://www.brookfieldreader.com

Brown Barn Books

119 Kettle Creek Road, Weston, CT 06883

Established:	2004	# of Employees:	–
Titles in Print:	–	Published Annually:	–

What They Publish

Publishes innovative crossover books for young adults age 12 and up.

Representative Titles/Projects

- *Running Horsemen*
- *Idiot!*
- *Home to the Sea*

Who They Hire

Authors/Writers:

Pays royalties/advances. Buys all rights.

Editors, proofreaders, illustrators, designers, production personnel:

Rates vary. Send cover letter with current résumé.

Internships/Summer Jobs:

Internships available: ☐ Yes ☒ No   Summer Jobs Available: ☐ Yes ☒ No

How to Get Connected

Contact:

Nancy Hammerslough, Editor in Chief

Accepts unsolicited/unagented manuscripts: ☒ Yes ☐ No
Accepts queries by: ☐ Email ☐ Fax ☐ Phone ☒ Letter
Query first. Responds if interested.

✉ Email: editorial@brownbarnbooks.com
🌐 Web Site: http://www.brownbarnbooks.com

Candlewick Press

2067 Massachusetts Avenue, Cambridge, MA 02140
(617) 661 3330

Established:	1991	# of Employees:	65
Titles in Print:	–	Published Annually:	–

What They Publish

Publishes young adult novels.

Representative Titles/Projects

- *Worm Gets a Job*
- *Pepo and Lolo and the Red Apple*
- *Tigress*

Who They Hire

Authors/Writers:
Pays royalties/advances. Buys all rights.

Editors, proofreaders, illustrators, designers, production personnel:
Rates vary. Send cover letter with current résumé.

Internships/Summer Jobs:
Internships available: ☐ Yes ☒ No   Summer Jobs Available: ☐ Yes ☒ No

How to Get Connected

Contact:
Deborah Wayshak, Karen Lotz, Elizabeth Bicknell, Editors

Accepts unsolicited/unagented manuscripts: ☐ Yes ☒ No
Accepts queries by: ☐ Email ☐ Fax ☐ Phone ☒ Letter
Publisher is not accepting unsolicited manuscripts at this time. Submission guidelines on website.

✉ Email: bigbear@candlewick.com
🌐 Web Site: http://www.candlewick.com

Capstone Press

PO Box 669, Mankato, MN 56002
(507) 345 8100

Established:	1991	# of Employees:	–
Titles in Print:	–	Published Annually:	400

What They Publish

Publishes nonfiction books for young readers Pre-K–12.

Representative Titles/Projects

- Famous Americans Series
- *Sleep Well: Why You Need Rest*
- *Endurance: Shipwreck and Survival on a Sea of Ice*

Who They Hire

Authors/Writers:
Pays royalties/advances. Buys all rights.

Editors, proofreaders, illustrators, designers, production personnel:
Rates vary. Send cover letter with current résumé.

Internships/Summer Jobs:
Internships available: ☐ Yes ☒ No   Summer Jobs Available: ☐ Yes ☒ No

How to Get Connected

Contact:
Publisher

Accepts unsolicited/unagented manuscripts: ☒ Yes   ☐ No
Accepts queries by: ☐ Email ☐ Fax ☐ Phone ☒ Letter
Query first. Responds if interested.

✉ Email:
🌐 Web Site: http://www.capstone-press.com

Carolrhoda Books

An Imprint of Lerner Publishing Group
241 First Avenue North, Minneapolis, MN 55401
(800) 328 4929

Established:	1959	# of Employees:	–
Titles in Print:	–	Published Annually:	–

What They Publish

Publishes high quality children's fiction and nonfiction.

Representative Titles/Projects

- *Mallory on the Move*
- *Rainbow Soup*
-

Who They Hire

Authors/Writers:
Pays royalties/advances. Buys all rights.

Editors, proofreaders, illustrators, designers, production personnel:
Rates vary. Send cover letter with current résumé.

Internships/Summer Jobs:
Internships available: ☐ Yes ☒ No   Summer Jobs Available: ☐ Yes ☒ No

How to Get Connected

Contact:
 Adam Lerner, Publisher

Accepts unsolicited/unagented manuscripts: ☒ Yes ☐ No
Accepts queries by: ☐ Email ☐ Fax ☐ Phone ☒ Letter
Query first. Responds if interested.

✉ Email:
🌐 Web Site: http://www.lernerbooks.com

Charlesbridge Publishing

85 Main Street, Watertown, MA 02172
(800) 225 3214

Established:	–	# of Employees:	–
Titles in Print:	–	Published Annually:	–

What They Publish

Publishes picture books and K–8 instruction materials.

Representative Titles/Projects

- *Candy Shop*
- *The Heroic Symphony*
- *Frog in a Bog*

Who They Hire

Authors/Writers:
Pays royalties/advances. Buys all rights.

Editors, proofreaders, illustrators, designers, production personnel:
Rates vary. Send cover letter with current résumé.

Internships/Summer Jobs:
Internships available: ☐ Yes ☒ No   Summer Jobs Available: ☐ Yes ☒ No

How to Get Connected

Contact:
Brent Farmer, Publisher
Harold Underdown, Editorial Director

Accepts unsolicited/unagented manuscripts: ☒ Yes ☐ No
Accepts queries by: ☐ Email ☐ Fax ☐ Phone ☒ Letter
Query first. Responds if interested.

✉ Email: books@charlesbridge.com
🌐 Web Site: http://www.charlesbridge.com

Chelsea House Publishers

2080 Cabot Boulevard West, Suite 201, Langhorne, PA 19047
(800) 848 BOOK

Established:	1970	# of Employees:	–
Titles in Print:	–	Published Annually:	–

What They Publish

Publishes library books for children and young adults, multicultural children's series, history, and biographies.

Representative Titles/Projects

- Religions of the World Series
- Modern World Nations Series
- Great Writers Series

Who They Hire

Authors/Writers:
Pays royalties/advances. Buys all rights.

Editors, proofreaders, illustrators, designers, production personnel:
Rates vary. Send cover letter with current résumé.

Internships/Summer Jobs:
Internships available: ☐ Yes ☒ No   Summer Jobs Available: ☐ Yes ☒ No

How to Get Connected

Contact:
Publisher

Accepts unsolicited/unagented manuscripts: ☒ Yes   ☐ No
Accepts queries by: ☐ Email ☐ Fax ☐ Phone ☒ Letter
Query first. Responds if interested.

✉ Email:
🌐 Web Site: http://www.chelseahouse.com

Chicago Review Press

814 N. Franklin Street, Chicago, Illinois 60610
(312) 337 0747

Established:	1973	# of Employees:	n/a
Titles in Print:	200	Published Annually:	35

What They Publish

Publishes nonfiction topics under three imprints:
* Chicago Review Press: general nonfiction and a growing line of children's' activity books.
* A Cappella Books: nonfiction, primarily on music.
* Lawrence Hill Books: progressive political and Black interest.

Representative Titles/Projects

* *American Revolution for Kids*, by Janis Herbert
* *When Race Becomes Real*, edited by Bernestine Singley
* *Snake Hips*, by Anne Thomas Soffee

Who They Hire

Writers:
Pays sliding royalty rate 7½ to 12½ percent/advances $2,000–$6,000. Retains all rights, but splits subsidiary rights.

Also assigns writers to prepare manuscripts for book concepts developed internally. Submit current résumé.

Copyeditors, proofreaders, and indexers:
All must be familiar with *The Chicago Manual of Style*. Rates negotiable. Submit current résumé.

Internships/Summer Jobs:
Internships available: ☒ Yes ☐ No   Summer Jobs Available: ☐ Yes   ☒ No

How to Get Connected

Contact:
Linda Matthews, Publisher
Cynthia Sherry, Acquisitions Editor, Chicago Review Press imprint manuscript queries
Gerilee Hundt, Managing Editor, all freelance inquiries

Accepts unsolicited/unagented manuscripts: ☒ Yes   ☐ No
Accepts queries by: ☐ Email ☐ Fax ☐ Phone ☒ Letter
Send query with outline and sample chapter. Must include an SASE. Do not send fiction, computer disks, or self-help manuscripts. Responds in 6–8 weeks.

✉ Email: csherry@ipgbook.com or publish@ipgbook.com (for mss queries only)
🌐 Web Site: http://www.ipgbook.com

Child and Family Press

440 First Street NW, 3rd Floor, Washington, DC 20001
(202) 638 2952

Established:	–	# of Employees:	–
Titles in Print:	–	Published Annually:	–

What They Publish

Publishes positive and entertaining children's titles and parenting titles that address families' issues and concerns.

Representative Titles/Projects

- *Every Child Deserves a Champion*
- *A Pocket Full of Kisses*
- *Taking the Plunge: A Teen's Guide to Independence*

Who They Hire

Authors/Writers:
Pays royalties/advances. Buys all rights.

Editors, proofreaders, illustrators, designers, production personnel:
Rates vary. Send cover letter with current résumé.

Internships/Summer Jobs:
Internships available: ☐ Yes ☒ No   Summer Jobs Available: ☐ Yes ☒ No

How to Get Connected

Contact:
Tegen Culler, Assistant Director of Publications

Accepts unsolicited/unagented manuscripts: ☒ Yes   ☐ No
Accepts queries by: ☐ Email ☐ Fax ☐ Phone ☒ Letter
Query first. Responds if interested.

✉ Email:
🌐 Web Site: http://www.cwla.org

Children's Book Press

2211 Mission Street, San Francisco, CA 94110

Established:	1975	# of Employees:	–
Titles in Print:	–	Published Annually:	–

What They Publish

Publishes multicultural and bilingual children's picture books.

Representative Titles/Projects

- *Featherless/Desplumado*
- *Cooper's Lesson*
- *The Barber's Cutting Edge*

Who They Hire

Authors/Writers:
Pays royalties/advances. Buys all rights.

Editors, proofreaders, illustrators, designers, production personnel:
Rates vary. Send cover letter with current résumé.

Internships/Summer Jobs:
Internships available: ☐ Yes ☒ No   Summer Jobs Available: ☐ Yes ☒ No

How to Get Connected

Contact:
Ina Cumpiano, Editorial Director

Accepts unsolicited/unagented manuscripts: ☒ Yes   ☐ No
Accepts queries by: ☐ Email ☐ Fax ☐ Phone ☒ Letter
Submission guidelines on website.

✉ Email: submissions@childrensbookpress.org
🌐 Web Site: http://www.childrensbookpress.org

Chronicle Books

85 Second Street, 6th Floor, San Francisco, CA 94105
(415) 537 4300

Established:	–	# of Employees:	–
Titles in Print:	–	Published Annually:	–

What They Publish

Publishes activity and storybooks for children.

Representative Titles/Projects

- *Doors*
- *Snug as a Bug*
- *Not So True Stories*

Who They Hire

Authors/Writers:
Pays royalties/advances. Buys all rights.

Editors, proofreaders, illustrators, designers, production personnel:
Rates vary. Send cover letter with current résumé.

Internships/Summer Jobs:
Internships available: ☐ Yes ☒ No   Summer Jobs Available: ☐ Yes ☒ No

How to Get Connected

Contact:
Victoria Rock, Director
Beth Weber, Managing Editor
Jennifer Vetter, Susan Pearson, Samantha McFerrin, Editors, Children's Books

Accepts unsolicited/unagented manuscripts: ☒ Yes ☐ No
Accepts queries by: ☐ Email ☐ Fax ☐ Phone ☒ Letter
Query first. Responds if interested.

✉ Email: frontdesk@chroniclebooks.com
🌐 Web Site: http://www.chroniclebooks.com

Clarion Books

An Imprint of Houghton Mifflin
215 Park Avenue South, New York, NY 10003

Established:	1965	# of Employees:	16
Titles in Print:	–	Published Annually:	50

What They Publish

Publishes children's books.

Representative Titles/Projects

- Curious George Series
- *The Firekeeper's Son*
- *Hot Potato*

Who They Hire

Authors/Writers:
Pays royalties/advances. Buys all rights.

Editors, proofreaders, illustrators, designers, production personnel:
Rates vary. Send cover letter with current résumé.

Internships/Summer Jobs:
Internships available: ☒ Yes ☐ No   Summer Jobs Available: ☐ Yes ☒ No

How to Get Connected

Contact:
Editorial Department

Accepts unsolicited/unagented manuscripts: ☒ Yes ☐ No
Accepts queries by: ☐ Email ☐ Fax ☐ Phone ☒ Letter

✉ Email:
🌐 Web Site: http://www.houghtonmifflinbooks.com/clarion

Cookie Bear Press

PO Box 5074, Buffalo Grove, IL 60089
(847) 955 0001

Established:	1987	# of Employees:	–
Titles in Print:	–	Published Annually:	–

What They Publish

Publishes children's books with unique themes.

Representative Titles/Projects

- *I Love You All the Time*
- *"I'm in the Bathroom!"*
-

Who They Hire

Authors/Writers:
Pays royalties. Buys all rights.

Editors, proofreaders, illustrators, designers, production personnel:
Rates vary. Send cover letter with current résumé.

Internships/Summer Jobs:
Internships available: ☐ Yes ☒ No   Summer Jobs Available: ☐ Yes ☒ No

How to Get Connected

Contact:
Jessica Elin Hirschman, Publisher

Accepts unsolicited/unagented manuscripts: ☒ Yes ☐ No
Accepts queries by: ☐ Email ☐ Fax ☐ Phone ☒ Letter
Query first. Responds if interested.

✉ Email: info@cookiebearpress.com
🌐 Web Site: http://www.cookiebearpress.com

Joanna Cotler Books

An Imprint of Harper Children's Books
10 East 53rd Street, New York, NY 10022
(212) 207 7541

Established:	–	# of Employees:	–
Titles in Print:	–	Published Annually:	–

What They Publish

Publishes literary and commercial picture books and fiction for all ages.

Representative Titles/Projects

- *Good Night Pillow Fight*
- *The Gospel Cinderella*
- *Bitte*

Who They Hire

Authors/Writers:
Pays royalties/advances. Buys all rights.

Editors, proofreaders, illustrators, designers, production personnel:
Rates vary. Send cover letter with current résumé.

Internships/Summer Jobs:
Internships available: ☒ Yes ☐ No   Summer Jobs Available: ☐ Yes ☒ No

How to Get Connected

Contact:
Joanna Cotler, Editor

Accepts unsolicited/unagented manuscripts: ☐ Yes   ☒ No
Accepts queries by: ☐ Email ☐ Fax ☐ Phone ☒ Letter
Query only. Responds if interested.

✉ Email:
🌐 Web Site: http://www.harpercollins.com

Creative Publishing International

18705 Lake East Drive, Chanhassen, MN 55317
(952) 936 4700

Established:	1969	# of Employees:	–
Titles in Print:	750	Published Annually:	–

What They Publish

Publishes under the imprints NorthWord (nature-themed books for young readers) and TwoCan (educational materials for ages 2–12).

Representative Titles/Projects

- *Good Morning, Garden*
- *Trout, Trout, Trout*
- Starting Life Series

Who They Hire

Authors/Writers:
Pays royalties/advances. Buys all rights.

Editors, proofreaders, illustrators, designers, production personnel:
Rates vary. Send cover letter with current résumé.

Internships/Summer Jobs:
Internships available: ☐ Yes ☒ No   Summer Jobs Available: ☐ Yes ☒ No

How to Get Connected

Contact:
Aimee Jackson, Executive Editor

Accepts unsolicited/unagented manuscripts: ☒ Yes ☐ No
Accepts queries by: ☐ Email ☐ Fax ☐ Phone ☒ Letter
Query first. Responds if interested.

✉ Email:
🌐 Web Site: http://www.creativepub.com

Cricket Books

An Imprint of Carus Publishing
PO Box 300, Peru IL 61354

Established:	1974	# of Employees:	–
Titles in Print:	–	Published Annually:	–

What They Publish

Publishes children's books for all ages.

Representative Titles/Projects

- *Double Dare to Be Scared*
- *Chief Sunrise*
- *Pigs Can Fly*

Who They Hire

Authors/Writers:
Pays royalties/advances. Buys all rights.

Editors, proofreaders, illustrators, designers, production personnel:
Rates vary. Send cover letter with current résumé.

Internships/Summer Jobs:
Internships available: ☒ Yes ☐ No   Summer Jobs Available: ☐ Yes ☒ No

How to Get Connected

Contact:
John Allen, Editor

Accepts unsolicited/unagented manuscripts: ☒ Yes ☐ No
Accepts queries by: ☐ Email ☐ Fax ☐ Phone ☒ Letter
Submission guidelines on website.

✉ Email:
🌐 Web Site: http://www.cricketmag.com

Crossway Books

Division of Good News Publishers

1300 Crescent Street, Wheaton, IL 60187
(630) 682 4300

Established:	1938	# of Employees:	50
Titles in Print:	350	Published Annually:	55

What They Publish

Publishes religious books from a conservative, evangelical Protestant point of view; fiction; and children's books with a Christian viewpoint for clergy, religious leaders, and lay leaders.

Representative Titles/Projects

- *The Holy Bible*, English Standard Version
- *The Roots of Endurance*, by John Piper
- *Disciplines of a Godly Man*, by R. Kent Hughes

Who They Hire

Writers:
Pays royalties, fees/advances against future royalties. Buys first North American and/or world book rights.

Editors, proofreaders, illustrators, designers, indexers, production personnel:
No freelance positions available at this time.

Internships/Summer Jobs:
Internships available: ☐ Yes ☒ No   Summer Jobs Available: ☐ Yes ☒ No

How to Get Connected

Contact:
Marvin Padgett, Vice President, Editorial

Accepts unsolicited/unagented manuscripts: ☒ Yes   ☐ No
Accepts queries by: ☐ Email ☐ Fax ☐ Phone ☒ Letter
Send query letter or manuscript. Must include an SASE. Do not phone or send ideas for picture books. Replies in 8–12 weeks.

✉ Email: n/a
🌐 Web Site: http://wwwcrosswaybooks.com

David Fickling Books

31 Beaumont Street, Oxford OX1 2NP, England
(0) 1865 339000

Established:	–	# of Employees:	–
Titles in Print:	–	Published Annually:	–

What They Publish

Publishes quality fiction and picture books for ages 0–18.

Note: This British publisher is included because Random House owns it and it is actively seeking manuscripts.

Representative Titles/Projects

- *Bing Make Music*
- *The Tale of Tales*
- *The Xenocide Mission*

Who They Hire

Authors/Writers:
Pays royalties/advances. Buys all rights.

Editors, proofreaders, illustrators, designers, production personnel:
n/a

Internships/Summer Jobs:
Internships available: ☐ Yes ☒ No   Summer Jobs Available: ☐ Yes ☒ No

How to Get Connected

Contact:
Acquisitions Editor

Accepts unsolicited/unagented manuscripts: ☒ Yes ☐ No
Accepts queries by: ☐ Email ☐ Fax ☐ Phone ☒ Letter
Send query letter with synopsis, first few chapters, and SASE (be sure you have international postage on the return).

✉ Email:
🌐 Web Site: http://www.davidficklingbooks.co.uk

Dawn Publications

12402 Bitney Springs Road, Nevada City, CA 95959
(530) 272 7775

Established:	1979	# of Employees:	5
Titles in Print:	–	Published Annually:	–

What They Publish

Publishes quality nature-awareness picture books for children.

Representative Titles/Projects

- *Ancient Rhymes: A Dolphin Lullaby*
- *Over in the Ocean*
- *Cat!*

Who They Hire

Authors/Writers:
Pays royalties/advances. Buys all rights.

Editors, proofreaders, illustrators, designers, production personnel:
Rates vary. Send cover letter with current résumé.

Internships/Summer Jobs:
Internships available: ☐ Yes ☒ No   Summer Jobs Available: ☐ Yes ☒ No

How to Get Connected

Contact:
Muffy Weaver, Co-Publisher
Glann Hovemann, Editor and Co-Publisher

Accepts unsolicited/unagented manuscripts: ☒ Yes ☐ No
Accepts queries by: ☐ Email ☐ Fax ☐ Phone ☒ Letter
Submission guidelines on website.

✉ Email:
🌐 Web Site: http://www.dawnpub.com

Delacorte Books for Young Readers

An Imprint of Random House
1745 Broadway, New York, NY 10019
(212) 782 9000

Established:	–	# of Employees:	–
Titles in Print:	–	Published Annually:	–

What They Publish

Publishes distinguished literary and commercial fiction for the middle grand and young adult markets.

Representative Titles/Projects

- *A Great and Terrible Beauty*
- The Edge Chronicles
- *Nate the Great*

Who They Hire

Authors/Writers:
Pays royalties/advances. Buys all rights.

Illustrators:
Rates vary. Send cover letter with current résumé, and samples. Samples returned if SASE included; otherwise kept on file. Responds only if interested. Pays by project or royalties. Original artwork returned at job's completion.

Internships/Summer Jobs:
Internships available: ☐ Yes ☒ No   Summer Jobs Available: ☐ Yes ☒ No

How to Get Connected

Contact:
Isabel Warren-Lynch, Executive Director, Art & Design

Accepts unsolicited/unagented manuscripts: ☐ Yes ☒ No
Accepts queries by: ☐ Email ☐ Fax ☐ Phone ☐ Letter
Although not currently accepting unsolicited manuscripts, manuscripts are being sought for two contests: Delecorte Dell Yearling Contest for a first middle-grade novel and Delacorte Press Contest for a first young adult novel. Submission guidelines can be found on website.

✉ Email:
🌐 Web Site: http://www.randomhouse.com/kids

Dial Books for Young Readers

An Imprint of Penguin Putnam
375 Hudson Street, New York, NY 10036
(212) 366 2000

Established:	1924	# of Employees:	–
Titles in Print:	–	Published Annually:	50

What They Publish

Publishes hardcover trade books for Kindergarten through young adult.

Representative Titles/Projects

- *We the Kids*
- *A Year Down Yonder*
- *A Long Way From Chicago*

Who They Hire

Authors/Writers:
Pays royalties/advances. Buys all rights.

Editors, proofreaders, illustrators, designers, production personnel:
Rates vary. Send cover letter with current résumé.

Internships/Summer Jobs:
Internships available: ☒ Yes ☐ No   Summer Jobs Available: ☐ Yes ☒ No

How to Get Connected

Contact:
Lauri Hornik, Associate Publisher and Editorial Director

Accepts unsolicited/unagented manuscripts: ☐ Yes ☐ No
Accepts queries by: ☐ Email ☐ Fax ☐ Phone ☒ Letter
Query only. Responds if interested.

✉ Email:
🌐 Web Site: http://www.penguinputnam.com

Disney Press

114 Fifth Avenue, New York, NY 10011
(212) 633 4400

Established:	–	# of Employees:	–
Titles in Print:	–	Published Annually:	–

What They Publish

Publishes children's books.

Representative Titles/Projects

- Lizzie McGuire Books
- Winnie the Pooh Books
- Disney Princess Books

Who They Hire

Authors/Writers:
Pays royalties/advances. Buys all rights.

Editors, proofreaders, illustrators, designers, production personnel:
Rates vary. Send cover letter with current résumé.

Internships/Summer Jobs:
Internships available: ☒ Yes ☐ No   Summer Jobs Available: ☐ Yes ☒ No

How to Get Connected

Contact:
Catherine Daly, Editorial Director
Liza Baker, Editor

Accepts unsolicited/unagented manuscripts: ☒ Yes ☐ No
Accepts queries by: ☐ Email ☐ Fax ☐ Phone ☒ Letter
Query first. Responds if interested.

✉ Email:
🌐 Web Site: http://www.disneybooks.com

Dogs in Hats Children's Publishing

PO Box 182, Grand Haven, MI 49417
(616) 844 2220

Established:	–	# of Employees:	–
Titles in Print:	–	Published Annually:	–

What They Publish

Publishes picture books and color and activity books.

Representative Titles/Projects

- Puppydog Tales Series
- Preschool Fun Books Series
- *Color By Number*

Who They Hire

Authors/Writers:
Pays royalties/advances. Buys all rights.

Editors, proofreaders, illustrators, designers, production personnel:
Rates vary. Send cover letter with current résumé.

Internships/Summer Jobs:
Internships available: ☐ Yes ☒ No   Summer Jobs Available: ☐ Yes ☒ No

How to Get Connected

Contact:
Peter Alfini, President

Accepts unsolicited/unagented manuscripts: ☒ Yes   ☐ No
Accepts queries by: ☒ Email ☐ Fax ☐ Phone ☐ Letter
Submission guidelines on website.

✉ Email: infodog@dogsinhats.com; submissions to john@dogsinhats.com
🌐 Web Site: http://www.dogsinhats.com

Dutton Children's Books

375 Hudson Street, New York, NY 10014
(212) 366 2000

Established:	1852	# of Employees:	–
Titles in Print:	–	Published Annually:	100

What They Publish

Publishes entertaining books for young readers.

Representative Titles/Projects

- *Wheels on the Bus*
- *Dinosaur Roar!*
- *Winnie the Pooh*

Who They Hire

Authors/Writers:
Pays royalties/advances. Buys all rights.

Editors, proofreaders, illustrators, designers, production personnel:
Rates vary. Send cover letter with current résumé.

Internships/Summer Jobs:
Internships available: ☒ Yes ☐ No   Summer Jobs Available: ☐ Yes ☒ No

How to Get Connected

Contact:
Stephanie Owens Lurie, Publisher
Alissa Heyman, Julie Strauss-Gabel, Lucia Monfried, Editors

Accepts unsolicited/unagented manuscripts: ☐ Yes ☒ No
Accepts queries by: ☐ Email ☐ Fax ☐ Phone ☒ Letter
Query only. Responds if interested.

✉ Email:
🌐 Web Site: http://www.penguinputnam.com

Eerdmans Books for Young Readers

255 Jefferson Avenue SE, Grand Rapids, MI 49503
(616) 459 4591

Established:	1911	# of Employees:	–
Titles in Print:	–	Published Annually:	–

What They Publish

Publishes books that nurture children's faith in God and help them understand the wonder, joy, and challenges of life.

Representative Titles/Projects

- *Going for the Record*
- *The Stolen Sun*
- *Adora*

Who They Hire

Authors/Writers:
Pays royalties/advances. Buys all rights.

Editors, proofreaders, illustrators, designers, production personnel:
Rates vary. Send cover letter with current résumé.

Internships/Summer Jobs:
Internships available: ☐ Yes ☒ No   Summer Jobs Available: ☐ Yes ☒ No

How to Get Connected

Contact:
Stephanie Owens Lurie, Publisher
Alissa Heyman, Julie Strauss-Gabel, Lucia Monfried, Editors

Accepts unsolicited/unagented manuscripts: ☒ Yes ☐ No
Accepts queries by: ☐ Email ☐ Fax ☐ Phone ☒ Letter
Submission guidelines on website.

✉ Email: youngreaders@eerdmans.com
🌐 Web Site: http://www.eerdmans.com/youngreaders

Encyclopedia Brittanica, Inc.

310 South Michigan Avenue, Chicago, IL 60604
(312) 347 7000

Established:	1878	# of Employees:	–
Titles in Print:	–	Published Annually:	–

What They Publish

Publishes educational reference material (encyclopedias, dictionaries, atlases, CD-ROMs).

Representative Titles/Projects

- *Encyclopedia Brittanica*
- *Encyclopedia Brittanica Online*

Who They Hire

Writers:
Pays royalties/advances. Buys all rights.

Editors, proofreaders, illustrators, designers, indexers, production personnel:
Rates vary. Send cover letter with current résumé.

Internships/Summer Jobs:
Internships available: ☒ Yes ☐ No   Summer Jobs Available: ☐ Yes ☒ No

How to Get Connected

Contact:
Dale Hoiberg, VP and Editor

Accepts unsolicited/unagented manuscripts: ☒ Yes ☐ No
Accepts queries by: ☐ Email ☐ Fax ☐ Phone ☒ Letter
Include an SASE with submission. Responds within 2 weeks.

✉ Email:
🌐 Web Site: http://www.eb.com

Everyday Learning Corporation

A Subsidiary of Tribune Education
2 Prudential Plaza, Suite 1200, Chicago, IL 60601
(312) 540 0210

Established:	1988	# of Employees:	105
Titles in Print:	135	Published Annually:	65

What They Publish

Publishes math, science, and social studies textbooks for kindergarten through twelfth grade and their teachers.

Currently looking for science topics.

Representative Titles/Projects

- *Everyday Mathematics, 2nd Edition*
- *Storypath*

Who They Hire

Writers:
Pays fees/advances. Retains all rights.

Copyeditors, proofreaders, indexers, designers, and artists:
Rates negotiable. Submit current résumé.

Internships/Summer Jobs:
Internships available: ☒ Yes ☐ No   Summer Jobs Available: ☐ Yes ☒ No

How to Get Connected

Contact:
Jo Anne Schiller, President and Publisher

Accepts unsolicited/unagented manuscripts: ☒ Yes ☐ No
Accepts queries by: ☐ Email ☐ Fax ☐ Phone ☒ Letter
Responds only when need arises.

✉ Email: elc-csr@tribune.com
🌐 Web Site: http://www.everydaylearning.com

Faith Kidz Books

Cook Communications Ministries
4050 Lee Vance View, Colorado Springs, CO 80918
(800) 708 5550

Established:	1875	# of Employees:	–
Titles in Print:	–	Published Annually:	–

What They Publish

Publishes children's books with Christian themes.

Representative Titles/Projects

- *Baby Bible ABC*
- God Prints Series
- Heaven and Mirth Series

Who They Hire

Authors/Writers:
Pays royalties/advances. Buys all rights.

Editors, proofreaders, illustrators, designers, production personnel:
Rates vary. Send cover letter with current résumé.

Internships/Summer Jobs:
Internships available: ☐ Yes ☒ No   Summer Jobs Available: ☐ Yes ☒ No

How to Get Connected

Contact:
Heather Gemmen, Associate Acquisitions Editor

Accepts unsolicited/unagented manuscripts: ☒ Yes ☐ No
Accepts queries by: ☐ Email ☐ Fax ☐ Phone ☒ Letter
Query first. Responds if interested.

✉ Email:
🌐 Web Site: http://www.cookministries.com

Farrar Straus Giroux Books for Young Readers

19 Union Square West, New York, NY 10003
(888) 330 8477

Established:	1946	# of Employees:	–
Titles in Print:	–	Published Annually:	–

What They Publish

Publishes books for toddlers through young adults.

Representative Titles/Projects

- *A Wrinkle in Time*
- *Tuck Everlasting*
- *The Cat Who Walked Across France*

Who They Hire

Authors/Writers:
Pays royalties/advances. Buys all rights.

Editors, proofreaders, illustrators, designers, production personnel:
Rates vary. Send cover letter with current résumé.

Internships/Summer Jobs:
Internships available: ☒ Yes ☐ No   Summer Jobs Available: ☐ Yes ☒ No

How to Get Connected

Contact:
Margaret Ferguson, Editorial Director, Books for Young Readers
Robbie Mayes, Editor, Books for Young Readers

Accepts unsolicited/unagented manuscripts: ☐ Yes ☐ No
Accepts queries by: ☒ Email ☐ Fax ☐ Phone ☒ Letter
Submission guidelines on website.

✉ Email: childresn.editorial@fsgbooks.com
🌍 Web Site: http://www.fsgbooks.com

Fireside

An Imprint of Simon & Schuster
1230 Avenue of the Americas, New York NY 10020

Established:	–	# of Employees:	–
Titles in Print:	–	Published Annually:	–

What They Publish

Publishes children's books.

Representative Titles/Projects

- *Birthday Bugs*
- Eliose Series
- Nancy Drew Girl Detective Series

Who They Hire

Authors/Writers:
Pays royalties/advances. Buys all rights.

Editors, proofreaders, illustrators, designers, production personnel:
Rates vary. Send cover letter with current résumé.

Internships/Summer Jobs:
Internships available: ☒ Yes ☐ No   Summer Jobs Available: ☐ Yes ☒ No

How to Get Connected

Contact:
Trish Todd, Editor

Accepts unsolicited/unagented manuscripts: ☐ Yes ☒ No
Accepts queries by: ☐ Email ☐ Fax ☐ Phone ☒ Letter
Query only. Responds if interested.

✉ Email:
🌐 Web Site: http://www.simonsayskids.com

Forest House Publishing Company, Inc.

PO Box 738, Lake Forest, IL 60045
(847) 295 8287

Established:	1989	# of Employees:	5
Titles in Print:	400	Published Annually:	30

What They Publish

Publishes school and library books—nonfiction, mystery, and concept books—for children in pre-kindergarten through seventh grade.

Currently looking for early math concept series: first and second grades only, full-color, not workbooks, but simple and clever ways to count and subtract.

Representative Titles/Projects

- *Alphabet Active Minds*
- *Matching*
- *Mystery of the Dragon in the Dungeon*

Who They Hire

Writers:
Uses freelance only. Pays royalties/small advances. Retains all rights.

Copyeditors, proofreaders, indexers, and designers:
Uses freelance only. Rates negotiable. Submit current résumé.

Internships/Summer Jobs:
Internships available: ☐ Yes ☒ No   Summer Jobs Available: ☐ Yes ☒ No

How to Get Connected

Contact:
Dianne Spahr, Co-Publisher and President
Roy Spahr, Publisher and Co-President

Accepts unsolicited/unagented manuscripts: ☒ Yes   ☐ No
Accepts queries by: ☐ Email ☐ Fax ☐ Phone ☒ Letter
Send query letter with a detailed plan for book or complete manuscript. Do not phone.
Responds within 12 months, earlier if interested. (They have a small staff, but attempt to respond as quickly as possible.)

✉ Email: info@forest-house.com
🌐 Web Site:

Free Spirit Publishing

217 Fifth Avenue North, Suite 200, Minneapolis, MN 55401
(612) 338 2068

Established:	1983	# of Employees:	–
Titles in Print:	–	Published Annually:	–

What They Publish

Publishes resources for educators, parents, and children regarding education, mental health, and social responsibility.

Representative Titles/Projects

- *Words Are Not For Hurting*
- *Our Family Meeting Book*
- *You're Smarter Than You Think*

Who They Hire

Authors/Writers:
Pays royalties/advances. Buys all rights.

Editors, proofreaders, illustrators, designers, production personnel:
Rates vary. Send cover letter with current résumé.

Internships/Summer Jobs:
Internships available: ☐ Yes ☒ No   Summer Jobs Available: ☐ Yes ☒ No

How to Get Connected

Contact:
Judy Galbraith, President

Accepts unsolicited/unagented manuscripts: ☒ Yes ☐ No
Accepts queries by: ☐ Email ☐ Fax ☐ Phone ☒ Letter
Submission guidelines on website.

✉ Email: help4kids@freespirit.com
🌐 Web Site: http://www.freespirit.com

Front Street Books

862 Haywood Road, Asheville, NC 28806
(828) 221 2091

Established:	–	# of Employees:	–
Titles in Print:	–	Published Annually:	–

What They Publish

Publishes books for children and young adults.

Representative Titles/Projects

- *The Nothing King*
- *Fair Monaco*
- *Hunger Moon*

Who They Hire

Authors/Writers:
Pays royalties/advances. Buys all rights.

Editors, proofreaders, illustrators, designers, production personnel:
Rates vary. Send cover letter with current résumé.

Internships/Summer Jobs:
Internships available: ☐ Yes ☒ No   Summer Jobs Available: ☐ Yes ☒ No

How to Get Connected

Contact:
Stephen Roxburgh, Publisher
Joyce Neaves, Editor

Accepts unsolicited/unagented manuscripts: ☒ Yes ☐ No
Accepts queries by: ☒ Email ☐ Fax ☐ Phone ☒ Letter
Email for queries only. Submission guidelines on website. Responds in 12 weeks.

✉ Email:
🌐 Web Site: http://www.frontstreetbooks.com

Gareth Stevens Inc.

330 West Olive Street, Suite 100, Milwaukee, WI 53212
(414) 332 3520

Established:	1983	# of Employees:	–
Titles in Print:	1,000	Published Annually:	200

What They Publish

Publishes educational books and high quality fiction for children ages 4–16.

Representative Titles/Projects

- *Let's Read About Pets*
- *Dave and the Tooth Fairy*
- *All About Wild Animals*

Who They Hire

Authors/Writers:
Pays royalties/advances. Buys all rights.

Editors, proofreaders, illustrators, designers, production personnel:
Rates vary. Send cover letter with current résumé.

Internships/Summer Jobs:
Internships available: ☐ Yes ☒ No   Summer Jobs Available: ☐ Yes ☒ No

How to Get Connected

Contact:
Gareth Stevens, Publisher

Accepts unsolicited/unagented manuscripts: ☒ Yes   ☐ No
Accepts queries by: ☐ Email ☐ Fax ☐ Phone ☒ Letter
Query first. Responds if interested.

✉ Email: info@gspubs.com
🌐 Web Site: http://www.garethstevens.com

Laura Geringer Books

An Imprint of Harper Collins
10 East 53rd Street, New York, NY 10022
(212) 207 7541

Established:	–	# of Employees:	–
Titles in Print:	–	Published Annually:	–

What They Publish

Publishes children's books.

Representative Titles/Projects

- *Toes*
- *So B. It*
-

Who They Hire

Authors/Writers:
Pays royalties/advances. Buys all rights.

Editors, proofreaders, illustrators, designers, production personnel:
Rates vary. Send cover letter with current résumé.

Internships/Summer Jobs:
Internships available: ☒ Yes ☐ No   Summer Jobs Available: ☐ Yes ☒ No

How to Get Connected

Contact:
Laura Geringer, Editor

Accepts unsolicited/unagented manuscripts: ☒ Yes   ☐ No
Accepts queries by: ☐ Email ☐ Fax ☐ Phone ☒ Letter
Query first. Responds if interested.

✉ Email:
🌐 Web Site: http://www.harpercollins.com

Golden Books Young Readers Group

An Imprint of Random House
1745 Broadway, New York NY 10019
(212) 782 9000

Established:	–	# of Employees:	–
Titles in Print:	–	Published Annually:	–

What They Publish

Publishes color and activity books; board and novelty books; fiction and nonfiction for beginning readers; and hardcover and paperback fiction for children ages 7 to young adult.

Representative Titles/Projects

- *Gross Encounters*
- Blue's Clues Series
-

Who They Hire

Authors/Writers:
Pays royalties/advances. Buys all rights.

Editors, proofreaders, illustrators, designers, production personnel:
Does not hire.

Internships/Summer Jobs:
Internships available: ☒ Yes ☐ No   Summer Jobs Available: ☐ Yes ☒ No

How to Get Connected

Contact:
Kate Klimo, Publisher
Mallory Loehr, Editor in Chief
Amy Jarashow, Associate Publisher
Cathy Goldsmith, Associate Publisher, Art Director

Accepts unsolicited/unagented manuscripts: ☐ Yes   ☒ No
Accepts queries by: ☐ Email ☐ Fax ☐ Phone ☐ Letter
Does not accept unsolicited manuscripts or queries. Works solely with agents.

✉ Email:
🌐 Web Site: http://www.randomhouse.com/kids

Goodheart-Willcox Company, Inc.

18604 West Creek Drive, Tinley Park, IL 60477
(708) 687 5000

Established:	1921	# of Employees:	63
Titles in Print:	140	Published Annually:	20

What They Publish

Publishes textbooks, workbooks, instructors' supplements, videos, and software programs for occupational/career and technological education, industrial and technical education, and family and consumer sciences for students in middle school through community college.

Representative Titles/Projects

- *Careers in Focus, Family & Consumer Services*, by Lee Jackson, CFCS
- *The World of Fashion Merchandising*, by Mary Wolfe
- *Building Life Skills*, by Louise A. Liddell, CFCS and Yvonne S. Gentzler, Ph.D.

Who They Hire

Writers:
Pays royalty ten percent of net income/seldom pays advances. Retains all rights. Authors should have teaching or industrial experience in the area in which they propose to write.

Editors, proofreaders, illustrators, designers, indexers, production personnel:
Rates vary. Send cover letter with current résumé.

Internships/Summer Jobs:
Internships available: ☒ Yes ☐ No   Summer Jobs Available: ☐ Yes ☒ No

How to Get Connected

Contact:
John Flanagan, President

Accepts unsolicited/unagented manuscripts: ☐ Yes ☒ No
Accepts queries by: ☐ Email ☐ Fax ☐ Phone ☒ Letter
Do not send unsolicited manuscripts. Responds to queries in 3 weeks.

✉ Email:
🌐 Web Site: http://www.goodheartwilcox.com

Grammy Time Books

PO Box 639, San Luis Obispo, CA 93406
(805) 541 3515

Established:	–	# of Employees:	–
Titles in Print:	–	Published Annually:	–

What They Publish

Publishes books that celebrate the grandparent, parent, and child relationships.

Representative Titles/Projects

- *Just You and Me*
- Reflection Series
- *Let's Make-Believe*

Who They Hire

Authors/Writers:
Pays royalties/advances. Buys all rights.

Editors, proofreaders, illustrators, designers, production personnel:
Rates vary. Send cover letter with current résumé.

Internships/Summer Jobs:
Internships available: ☐ Yes ☒ No   Summer Jobs Available: ☐ Yes ☒ No

How to Get Connected

Contact:
Stephanie Hicks, President and Publisher
P. Taylor Copeland, Publisher

Accepts unsolicited/unagented manuscripts: ☒ Yes ☐ No
Accepts queries by: ☐ Email ☐ Fax ☐ Phone ☒ Letter
Query first. Responds if interested.

✉ Email: Stephanie@grammytimebooks.com
🌐 Web Site: http://www.grammytimebooks.com

Graphia Books

An Imprint of Houghton Mifflin
215 Park Avenue South, New York, NY 10003

Established:	–	# of Employees:	–
Titles in Print:	–	Published Annually:	–

What They Publish

Publishes novels for teens.

Representative Titles/Projects

- *Owl in Love*
- *Comfort*
- *48 Shades of Brown*

Who They Hire

Authors/Writers:
Pays royalties/advances. Buys all rights.

Editors, proofreaders, illustrators, designers, production personnel:
Rates vary. Send cover letter with current résumé.

Internships/Summer Jobs:
Internships available: ☐ Yes ☒ No   Summer Jobs Available: ☐ Yes ☒ No

How to Get Connected

Contact:
Editor

Accepts unsolicited/unagented manuscripts: ☒ Yes ☐ No
Accepts queries by: ☐ Email ☐ Fax ☐ Phone ☒ Letter
Query first. Responds if interested.

✉ Email:
🌐 Web Site: http://www.houghtonmifflinbooks.com

Green Tiger Press

An Imprint of Laughing Elephant
3645 Interlake Avenue North, Seattle, WA 98103
(206) 447 9229

Established:	1969	# of Employees:	–
Titles in Print:	–	Published Annually:	–

What They Publish

Publishes children's books and note cards.

Representative Titles/Projects

- *The Black Cat Book*
- *Starcleaner Reunion*
- *The Catalog*

Who They Hire

Editors, proofreaders, production personnel:
Rates vary. Send cover letter with current résumé.

Internships/Summer Jobs:
Internships available: ☐ Yes ☒ No   Summer Jobs Available: ☐ Yes ☒ No

How to Get Connected

Contact:
Harold and Sandra Darling, Publishers
Abigail Darling, Editor

Accepts unsolicited/unagented manuscripts: ☐ Yes   ☒ No
Accepts queries by: ☐ Email ☐ Fax ☐ Phone ☐ Letter
The publisher does not accept manuscript or illustration submissions of any kind. All work done in house.

✉ Email:
🌐 Web Site: http://www.laughingelephant.com

Greenwillow Books

An Imprint of Harper Collins
1350 Avenue of the Americas, New York NY 10019
(212) 261 6500

Established:	1974	# of Employees:	–
Titles in Print:	–	Published Annually:	–

What They Publish

Publishes books for children of every age.

Representative Titles/Projects

- *North*
- *Feverbird's Claw*
- *Unexpected Magic*

Who They Hire

Authors/Writers:
Pays royalties/advances. Buys all rights.

Editors, proofreaders, illustrators, designers, production personnel:
Rates vary. Send cover letter with current résumé.

Internships/Summer Jobs:
Internships available: ☒ Yes ☐ No   Summer Jobs Available: ☐ Yes ☒ No

How to Get Connected

Contact:
Rebecca Davis, Senior Editor
Steve Geck, Editor

Accepts unsolicited/unagented manuscripts: ☐ Yes ☒ No
Accepts queries by: ☐ Email ☐ Fax ☐ Phone ☒ Letter
Query only. Responds if interested.

✉ Email:
🌐 Web Site: http://www.harperchildrens.com

Grosset & Dunlap

An Imprint of Penguin Putnam
375 Hudson Street, New York NY 10014
(212) 366 2000

Established:	1898	# of Employees:	–
Titles in Print:	–	Published Annually:	–

What They Publish

Publishes books of originality, quality, and value for children grades K–12.

Representative Titles/Projects

- *Smart About Art*
- All Aboard Reading Series
- Who Was …? Series

Who They Hire

Authors/Writers:
Pays royalties/advances. Buys all rights.

Editors, proofreaders, illustrators, designers, production personnel:
Rates vary. Send cover letter with current résumé.

Internships/Summer Jobs:
Internships available: ☒ Yes ☐ No   Summer Jobs Available: ☐ Yes ☒ No

How to Get Connected

Contact:
Debra Dorfman, President and Publisher
Bonnie Bader, Editorial Director
Debra Dorfman, Editor

Accepts unsolicited/unagented manuscripts: ☐ Yes   ☒ No
Accepts queries by: ☐ Email ☐ Fax ☐ Phone ☒ Letter
Query only. Responds if interested.

✉ Email:
🌐 Web Site: http://www.penguinputnam.com

Gryphon House

PO Box 207, Beltsville, MD 20704
(301) 595 9500

Established:	1971	# of Employees:	–
Titles in Print:	–	Published Annually:	–

What They Publish

Publishes early childhood books for teachers and parents.

Representative Titles/Projects

- *Bilingual Book of Rhymes, Stores and Fingerplays*
- *Learning Power of Laughter*
- *Zen Parenting*

Who They Hire

Authors/Writers:
Pays royalties/advances. Buys all rights.

Editors, proofreaders, illustrators, designers, production personnel:
Rates vary. Send cover letter with current résumé.

Internships/Summer Jobs:
Internships available: ☐ Yes ☒ No   Summer Jobs Available: ☐ Yes ☒ No

How to Get Connected

Contact:
Leah Curry-Rood, Editor

Accepts unsolicited/unagented manuscripts: ☒ Yes ☐ No
Accepts queries by: ☐ Email ☐ Fax ☐ Phone ☒ Letter
Query first. Responds if interested.

✉ Email:
🕭 Web Site: http://www.gryphonhouse.com

Handprint Books

413 Sixth Avenue, Brooklyn, NY 11215
(718) 768 3696

Established:	1975	# of Employees:	–
Titles in Print:	–	Published Annually:	–

What They Publish

Publishes good books for children.

Representative Titles/Projects

- *Bless This Mouse*
- *Petropolis*
- *Noisy City Day*

Who They Hire

Authors/Writers:
Pays royalties/advances. Buys all rights.

Editors, proofreaders, illustrators, designers, production personnel:
Rates vary. Send cover letter with current résumé.

Internships/Summer Jobs:
Internships available: ☐ Yes ☒ No   Summer Jobs Available: ☐ Yes ☒ No

How to Get Connected

Contact:
Christopher Franceschelli, Publisher
Ann Tobias, Executive Editor
Gina Scauzillo, Managing Editor

Accepts unsolicited/unagented manuscripts: ☒ Yes ☐ No
Accepts queries by: ☐ Email ☐ Fax ☐ Phone ☒ Letter
Submission guidelines on website. Responds in 8–10 weeks.

✉ Email: anntobias@handprintbooks.com
🌐 Web Site: http://www.handprintbooks.com

Harcourt Children's Books

525 B Street, Suite 1900, San Diego, CA 92101
(619) 231 6616

Established:	1919	# of Employees:	–
Titles in Print:	–	Published Annually:	–

What They Publish

Publishes books for young readers through teens.

Representative Titles/Projects

- *How I Became a Pirate*
- *Ginger Pye*
- *What Happened to Lori Garver*

Who They Hire

Authors/Writers:
Pays royalties/advances. Buys all rights.

Editors, proofreaders, illustrators, designers, production personnel:
Rates vary. Send cover letter with current résumé.

Internships/Summer Jobs:
Internships available: ☒ Yes ☐ No   Summer Jobs Available: ☐ Yes ☒ No

How to Get Connected

Contact:
Allyn Johnston, Editorial Director
Michael Stearns, Jeanette Larson, Editors

Accepts unsolicited/unagented manuscripts: ☐ Yes ☐ No
Accepts queries by: ☐ Email ☐ Fax ☐ Phone ☒ Letter
Submission guidelines on website.

✉ Email:
🌐 Web Site: http://www.harcourtbooks.com

Harper Children's Books

1350 Avenue of the Americas, New York NY 10019
(212) 261 6500

Established:	–	# of Employees:	–
Titles in Print:	–	Published Annually:	–

What They Publish

Publishes children's books.

Representative Titles/Projects

- *Princess Lessons*
- *Moo Who?*
- *Daddy All Day Long*

Who They Hire

Authors/Writers:
Pays royalties/advances. Buys all rights.

Editors, proofreaders, illustrators, designers, production personnel:
Rates vary. Send cover letter with current résumé.

Internships/Summer Jobs:
Internships available: ☒ Yes ☐ No   Summer Jobs Available: ☐ Yes ☒ No

How to Get Connected

Contact:
Maria Modugno, Vice President and Editorial Director
Alix Reid, Phoebe Yeh, Editorial Directors
Kate Morgan Jackson, Editor in Chief
Ruth Katcher, Senior Editor
Marjorie, Braman, Jodi Harris, Clarissa Hutton, Barbara Lalicki, Amanda Maciel, Antonia Markiet,
Abby McAden, Susan Rich, Katherine Brown Tegen, Tara Weikum, Editors

Accepts unsolicited/unagented manuscripts: ☐ Yes ☒ No
Accepts queries by: ☐ Email ☐ Fax ☐ Phone ☒ Letter
Query only. Responds if interested.

✉ Email:
🌐 Web Site: http://www.harperchildrens.com

Harper Festival

1350 Avenue of the Americas, New York, NY 10019
(212) 261 6500

Established:	–	# of Employees:	–
Titles in Print:	–	Published Annually:	–

What They Publish

Publishes books, novelties, and merchandise for the very young (ages 0–6).

Representative Titles/Projects

- *Runaway Bunny*
- *Harold and the Purple Crayon: Shapes*
- *Goodnight Moon*

Who They Hire

Authors/Writers:
Pays royalties/advances. Buys all rights.

Editors, proofreaders, illustrators, designers, production personnel:
Rates vary. Send cover letter with current résumé.

Internships/Summer Jobs:
Internships available: ☒ Yes ☐ No   Summer Jobs Available: ☐ Yes ☒ No

How to Get Connected

Contact:
Emily Brenner, Editorial Director

Accepts unsolicited/unagented manuscripts: ☐ Yes ☒ No
Accepts queries by: ☐ Email ☐ Fax ☐ Phone ☒ Letter
Query only. Responds if interested.

✉ Email:
🌐 Web Site: http://www.harperchildrens.com

Harper Trophy

1350 Avenue of the Americas, New York, NY 10019
(212) 261 6500

Established:	–	# of Employees:	–
Titles in Print:	–	Published Annually:	–

What They Publish

Harper Trophy is the premier paperback imprint for children.

Representative Titles/Projects

- *Always Wear Clean Underwear*
- *Who Was That Masked Man, Anyway?*
- *The Creek*

Who They Hire

Authors/Writers:
Pays royalties/advances. Buys all rights.

Editors, proofreaders, illustrators, designers, production personnel:
Rates vary. Send cover letter with current résumé.

Internships/Summer Jobs:
Internships available: ☒ Yes ☐ No   Summer Jobs Available: ☐ Yes ☒ No

How to Get Connected

Contact:
Editorial Director

Accepts unsolicited/unagented manuscripts: ☐ Yes   ☒ No
Accepts queries by: ☐ Email ☐ Fax ☐ Phone ☒ Letter
Query only. Responds if interested.

✉ Email:
🌐 Web Site: http://www.harperchildrens.com

Henry Holt Books for Young Readers

115 West 18th Street, New York NY 10011
(212) 886 9332

Established:	–	# of Employees:	–
Titles in Print:	–	Published Annually:	–

What They Publish

Publishes children's books.

Representative Titles/Projects

- *The Beach Patrol*
- *Dumpy LaRue*
- *The Shamer's Daughter*

Who They Hire

Authors/Writers:
Pays royalties/advances. Buys all rights.

Editors, proofreaders, illustrators, designers, production personnel:
Rates vary. Send cover letter with current résumé.

Internships/Summer Jobs:
Internships available: ☒ Yes ☐ No   Summer Jobs Available: ☐ Yes ☒ No

How to Get Connected

Contact:
Laura Godwin, Vice President
Kate Farrell, Christy Ottaviano, Editors

Accepts unsolicited/unagented manuscripts: ☐ Yes ☒ No
Accepts queries by: ☐ Email ☐ Fax ☐ Phone ☒ Letter
Query only. Responds if interested.

✉ Email:
🌐 Web Site: http://www.henryholt.com

Holiday House

425 Madison Avenue, New York NY 10017

Established:	–	# of Employees:	–
Titles in Print:	–	Published Annually:	–

What They Publish

Publishes quality fiction and nonfiction hardcover books from the picture book level to young adult.

Representative Titles/Projects

- *Bug Safari*
- *The Double-Digit Club*
- *Follow the Blue*

Who They Hire

Authors/Writers:

Pays royalties/advances. Buys all rights.

Editors, proofreaders, illustrators, designers, production personnel:

Rates vary. Send cover letter with current résumé.

Internships/Summer Jobs:

Internships available: ☐ Yes ☒ No   Summer Jobs Available: ☐ Yes ☒ No

How to Get Connected

Contact:

Mary Cash, Editor

Accepts unsolicited/unagented manuscripts: ☒ Yes ☐ No
Accepts queries by: ☐ Email ☐ Fax ☐ Phone ☒ Letter
Submission guidelines on website. Responds in 8 weeks.

✉ Email:
🌐 Web Site: http://www.holidayhouse.com

Houghton Mifflin Children's Books

222 Berkeley Street, Boston, MA 02116
(617) 351 3668

Established:	–	# of Employees:	–
Titles in Print:	–	Published Annually:	–

What They Publish

Publishes children's books.

Representative Titles/Projects

- *Ollie the Stomper*
- *Henry Climbs a Mountain*
- Curious George Series

Who They Hire

Authors/Writers:
Pays royalties/advances. Buys all rights.

Editors, proofreaders, illustrators, designers, production personnel:
Rates vary. Send cover letter with current résumé.

Internships/Summer Jobs:
Internships available: ☒ Yes ☐ No   Summer Jobs Available: ☐ Yes ☒ No

How to Get Connected

Contact:
Judy O'Malley, Editorial Director
Margaret Raymo, Edxecutive Editor
Ann Rider, Senior Editor
Andrea Davis Pinkney, Eden Edwards, Amy Flynn (middle-grade novels), Kate O'Sullivan, Editors
Hanna Rodgers, Submissions Coordinator

Accepts unsolicited/unagented manuscripts: ☐ Yes   ☒ No
Accepts queries by: ☐ Email ☐ Fax ☐ Phone ☒ Letter
Query only. Responds if interested.

✉ Email: childrens_books@hmco.com
🌐 Web Site: http://www.houghtonmifflinbooks.com

Hyperion Books for Children

114 Fifth Avenue, New York, NY 10011
(212) 633 4400

Established:	1991	# of Employees:	–
Titles in Print:	–	Published Annually:	–

What They Publish

Publishes imaginative and though-provoking literature for children.

Representative Titles/Projects

- *What Is Goodbye?*
- *Sign of the Qin*
- *McDuff's Favorite Things*

Who They Hire

Authors/Writers:
Pays royalties/advances. Buys all rights.

Editors, proofreaders, illustrators, designers, production personnel:
Rates vary. Send cover letter with current résumé.

Internships/Summer Jobs:
Internships available: ☒ Yes ☐ No   Summer Jobs Available: ☐ Yes ☒ No

How to Get Connected

Contact:
Liza Baker, Editorial Director
Alessandra Balzer, Helen Perelman, Executive Editors
Donna Bray, Wendy Lefkon, Editors

Accepts unsolicited/unagented manuscripts: ☐ Yes ☒ No
Accepts queries by: ☐ Email ☐ Fax ☐ Phone ☐ Letter

✉ Email:
🌐 Web Site: http://www.hyperionbooksforchildren.com

Ideals Publications

535 Metroplex Drive, #250, Nashville, TN 37211
(615) 333 0478

Established:	1947	# of Employees:	–
Titles in Print:	–	Published Annually:	–

What They Publish

Publishes books for 3–10 year olds under the imprints Candy Cane Press and Ideals Children's Books.

Representative Titles/Projects

- *Thank You, God*
- *The Story of America's Birthday*
- *The Littlest Angel*

Who They Hire

Authors/Writers:

Pays royalties/advances. Buys all rights.

Editors, proofreaders, illustrators, designers, production personnel:

Rates vary. Send cover letter with current résumé.

Internships/Summer Jobs:

Internships available: ☐ Yes ☒ No   Summer Jobs Available: ☐ Yes ☒ No

How to Get Connected

Contact:

Patricia Pingry, Publisher
Peggy Schaefer, Managing Editor

Accepts unsolicited/unagented manuscripts: ☒ Yes ☐ No
Accepts queries by: ☐ Email ☐ Fax ☐ Phone ☒ Letter
Query first. Responds if interested.

✉ Email:
🌐 Web Site: http://www.idealspublications.com

Illumination Arts

PO Box 1865, Bellevue, WA 98009
(425) 644 7185

Established:	1987	# of Employees:	–
Titles in Print:	–	Published Annually:	–

What They Publish

Publishes children's books on New Age topics.

Representative Titles/Projects

- *The Bonsai Bear*
- *All I See Is Part of Me*
- *Dreambirds*

Who They Hire

Authors/Writers:
Pays royalties/advances. Buys all rights.

Editors, proofreaders, illustrators, designers, production personnel:
Rates vary. Send cover letter with current résumé.

Internships/Summer Jobs:
Internships available: ☐ Yes ☒ No   Summer Jobs Available: ☐ Yes ☒ No

How to Get Connected

Contact:
Ruth Thompson, Editorial Director

Accepts unsolicited/unagented manuscripts: ☒ Yes ☐ No
Accepts queries by: ☐ Email ☐ Fax ☐ Phone ☒ Letter
Query first. Responds if interested.

✉ Email: liteinfo@illumin.com
🌐 Web Site: http://www.illumin.com

Innovative Kids

18 Ann Street, Norwalk, CT 06870
(203) 838 6400

Established:	–	# of Employees:	–
Titles in Print:	–	Published Annually:	–

What They Publish

Publishes hands-on, interactive, educational children's books.

Representative Titles/Projects

- *Code Masters: Rain Forest Adventures*
- Now I'm Reading Series
- Memory Match Game Books

Who They Hire

Authors/Writers:
Pays royalties/advances. Buys all rights.

Editors, proofreaders, illustrators, designers, production personnel:
Rates vary. Send cover letter with current résumé.

Internships/Summer Jobs:
Internships available: ☐ Yes ☒ No   Summer Jobs Available: ☐ Yes ☒ No

How to Get Connected

Contact:
Shari Kaufman, President

Accepts unsolicited/unagented manuscripts: ☒ Yes ☐ No
Accepts queries by: ☐ Email ☐ Fax ☐ Phone ☒ Letter
Submission guidelines on website. Responds in 8–10 weeks.

✉ Email: info@innovativekids.com
🌐 Web Site: http://www.innovativekids.com

Richard Jackson Books

An Imprint of Atheneum Books for Young Readers
1230 Avenue of the Americas, New York, NY 10020

Established: –   # of Employees: –
Titles in Print: –   Published Annually: –

What They Publish

Publishes children's books.

Representative Titles/Projects

- *Birthday Bugs*
- *The AuPairs*
- Nancy Drew Girl Detective Series

Who They Hire

Authors/Writers:
Pays royalties/advances. Buys all rights.

Editors, proofreaders, illustrators, designers, production personnel:
Rates vary. Send cover letter with current résumé.

Internships/Summer Jobs:
Internships available: ☒ Yes ☐ No   Summer Jobs Available: ☐ Yes ☒ No

How to Get Connected

Contact:
Richard Jackson, Editor

Accepts unsolicited/unagented manuscripts: ☐ Yes   ☒ No
Accepts queries by: ☐ Email ☐ Fax ☐ Phone ☒ Letter
Query only. Responds if interested.

✉ Email:
🜨 Web Site: http://www.simonsayskids.com

Just Us Books

356 Glenwood Avenue, East Orange, NJ 01017
(973) 672 7701

Established:	1988	# of Employees:	–
Titles in Print:	–	Published Annually:	–

What They Publish

Publishes children's books and learning materials from the Black experience.

Representative Titles/Projects

- *Brown Eyes, Brown Skin*
- *Annie's Gift*
- *AFRO-BETS® ABC Book*

Who They Hire

Authors/Writers:
Pays royalties/advances. Buys all rights.

Editors, proofreaders, illustrators, designers, production personnel:
Rates vary. Send cover letter with current résumé.

Internships/Summer Jobs:
Internships available: ☐ Yes ☒ No   Summer Jobs Available: ☐ Yes ☒ No

How to Get Connected

Contact:
Cheryl Hudson, Editor
Katura Hudson, Associate Editor

Accepts unsolicited/unagented manuscripts: ☒ Yes ☐ No
Accepts queries by: ☐ Email ☐ Fax ☐ Phone ☒ Letter
Submission guidelines on website. Responds in 8–10 weeks.

✉ Email: justusbook@mindspring.com
🌐 Web Site: http://www.justusbooks.com

Katherine Tegen Books

An Imprint of Harper Children's Books
1350 Avenue of the Americas, New York, NY 10019
(212) 261 6500

Established:	–	# of Employees:	–
Titles in Print:	–	Published Annually:	–

What They Publish

Publishes stories created from memorable characters and fresh voices.

Representative Titles/Projects

- *Moo Who?*
- *Amelia's Show and Tell Fiesta*
- *Wallace's List*

Who They Hire

Authors/Writers:
Pays royalties/advances. Buys all rights.

Editors, proofreaders, illustrators, designers, production personnel:
Rates vary. Send cover letter with current résumé.

Internships/Summer Jobs:
Internships available: ☒ Yes ☐ No   Summer Jobs Available: ☐ Yes ☒ No

How to Get Connected

Contact:
Katherine Tegen, Editorial Director

Accepts unsolicited/unagented manuscripts: ☐ Yes   ☒ No
Accepts queries by: ☐ Email ☐ Fax ☐ Phone ☒ Letter
Query only. Responds if interested.

✉ Email:
🌐 Web Site: http://www.harperchildrens.com

Kazi Publications, Inc.

3023 W. Belmont Avenue, Chicago, IL 60618
(773) 267 7001

Established:	1976	# of Employees:	1
Titles in Print:	350	Published Annually:	12

What They Publish

Publishes nonfiction and fiction about Islam, Islamic culture and civilization, and the Middle East for children and adults.

Representative Titles/Projects

- *What Everyone Should Know About Islam and Muslims*
- *Ideals and Realities in Islam*
- *Sufi Women of America: Angels in the Making*

Who They Hire

Writers:
Pays ten percent royalty/advances. Author retains copyright.

Copyeditors and manuscript readers:
Rates negotiable. Submit current résumé.

Internships/Summer Jobs:
Internships available: ☐ Yes ☒ No   Summer Jobs Available: ☐ Yes ☒ No

How to Get Connected

Contact:
Mary Bakhitiar

Accepts unsolicited/unagented manuscripts: ☒ Yes ☐ No
Accepts queries by: ☐ Email ☐ Fax ☐ Phone ☒ Letter
Responds in 4 weeks.

✉ Email: info@kazi.org
🌐 Web Site: http://www.kazi.org

Kids Can Press

2250 Military Road, Tonawanda, NY 14150
(866) 481 5827

Established:	1973	# of Employees:	42
Titles in Print:	350	Published Annually:	–

What They Publish

Publishes picture books, young adult fiction, science, nature, crafts, and activity books.

Representative Titles/Projects

- *The Biggest Fish in the Lake*
- Franklin the Turtle® Series
- *The Thought of High Windows*

Who They Hire

Authors/Writers:
Pays royalties/advances. Buys all rights.

Editors, proofreaders, illustrators, designers, production personnel:
Rates vary. Send cover letter with current résumé.

Internships/Summer Jobs:
Internships available: ☐ Yes ☒ No   Summer Jobs Available: ☐ Yes ☒ No

How to Get Connected

Contact:
Editor

Accepts unsolicited/unagented manuscripts: ☐ Yes ☒ No
Accepts queries by: ☐ Email ☐ Fax ☐ Phone ☐ Letter
Submission guidelines on website.

✉ Email:
🌐 Web Site: http://www.kidscanpress.com

KidsBooks, Inc.

230 Fifth Avenue, Suite 1710, New York, NY 10001
(212) 685 4444

Established:	1987	# of Employees:	–
Titles in Print:	300	Published Annually:	100

What They Publish

Publishes fiction and nonfiction books, activity books, a nature series, a how-to-draw series, and trivia fun.

Representative Titles/Projects

- *The Creepiest, Scariest, Weirdest Creatures Ever!*
- *Wake Up, Night*
- *Fantasy Cars*

Who They Hire

Authors/Writers:
Pays royalties/advances. Buys all rights.

Editors, proofreaders, illustrators, designers, production personnel:
Rates vary. Send cover letter with current résumé.

Internships/Summer Jobs:
Internships available: ☒ Yes ☐ No   Summer Jobs Available: ☐ Yes ☒ No

How to Get Connected

Contact:
Vic Cavallaro, Publisher

Accepts unsolicited/unagented manuscripts: ☐ Yes ☒ No
Accepts queries by: ☐ Email ☐ Fax ☐ Phone ☐ Letter
Submission guidelines on website. Responds if interested.

✉ Email:
🌐 Web Site: http://www.kidsbooks.com

Kingfisher

An Imprint of Houghton Mifflin
215 Park Avenue South, New York, NY 10003

Established:	–	# of Employees:	–
Titles in Print:	–	Published Annually:	–

What They Publish

Publishes nonfiction for K–9th grades.

Representative Titles/Projects

- *Robots*
- *Mummies*
- *The Great Art Scandal*

Who They Hire

Authors/Writers:
Pays royalties/advances. Buys all rights.

Editors, proofreaders, illustrators, designers, production personnel:
Rates vary. Send cover letter with current résumé.

Internships/Summer Jobs:
Internships available: ☒ Yes ☐ No   Summer Jobs Available: ☐ Yes ☒ No

How to Get Connected

Contact:
Editor

Accepts unsolicited/unagented manuscripts: ☐ Yes ☒ No
Accepts queries by: ☐ Email ☐ Fax ☐ Phone ☒ Letter
Query only. Responds if interested.

✉ Email:
🌐 Web Site: http://www.houghtonmifflinbooks.com

Alfred A. Knopf and Crown Books for Young Readers

An Imprint of Random House
1745 Broadway, 9–3, New York, NY 10019
(212) 782 9000

Established:	–	# of Employees:	–
Titles in Print:	–	Published Annually:	–

What They Publish

Publishes distinguished juvenile fiction and nonfiction for ages 0–18.

Representative Titles/Projects

- *Pinky Dinky Doo*
- Junie B. Jones Series
- *The Amber Spyglass*

Who They Hire

Authors/Writers:
Pays royalties/advances. Buys all rights.

Illustrators:
Rates vary. Send cover letter with current résumé and samples. Samples will be returned if SASE is included; otherwise kept on file. Responds only if interested. Pays by project or royalties. Original artwork returned at job's completion.

Internships/Summer Jobs:
Internships available: ☐ Yes ☒ No   Summer Jobs Available: ☐ Yes ☒ No

How to Get Connected

Contact:
Acquisitions Editor
Isabel Warren-Lynch, Executive Director, Art & Design

Accepts unsolicited/unagented manuscripts: ☒ Yes ☐ No
Accepts queries by: ☐ Email ☐ Fax ☐ Phone ☒ Letter
Query first. Send query letter with SASE for response.

✉ Email:
🌐 Web Site: http://www.randomhouse.com/kids

Kregel Publications

PO Box 2607, Grand Rapids, MI 49501
(616) 451 4775

Established:	1949	# of Employees:	–
Titles in Print:	600	Published Annually:	–

What They Publish

Publishes Christian books for young adults.

Representative Titles/Projects

- *God's Front Door*
- *The Wonderful World That God Made*
-

Who They Hire

Authors/Writers:
Pays royalties/advances. Buys all rights.

Editors, proofreaders, illustrators, designers, production personnel:
Rates vary. Send cover letter with current résumé.

Internships/Summer Jobs:
Internships available: ☐ Yes ☒ No   Summer Jobs Available: ☐ Yes ☒ No

How to Get Connected

Contact:
Dennis Hillman, Publisher

Accepts unsolicited/unagented manuscripts: ☒ Yes   ☐ No
Accepts queries by: ☐ Email ☐ Fax ☐ Phone ☒ Letter
Submission guidelines on website.

✉ Email: editorial@kregel.com
🌐 Web Site: http://www.kregel.com

Wendy Lamb Books

An Imprint of Random House Children's Books
1745 Broadway, New York, NY 10019
(212) 782 9000

Established:	–	# of Employees:	–
Titles in Print:	–	Published Annually:	12

What They Publish

Publishes literary fiction and nonfiction for readers 8–12 and 12–15.

Representative Titles/Projects

- *Charlotte's Rose*
- *Pictures of Hollis Woods*
-

Who They Hire

Authors/Writers:
Pays royalties. Buys all rights.

Illustrators:
Rates vary. Send cover letter with current résumé and samples. Responds only if interested. Pays by project or royalties. Original artwork returned at job's completion.

Internships/Summer Jobs:
Internships available: ☒ Yes ☐ No   Summer Jobs Available: ☐ Yes ☒ No

How to Get Connected

Contact:
Wendy Lamb, Editor Director and Acquisitions Editor
Alison Root, Editor
Isabel Warren-Lynch, Executive Director, Art & Design

Accepts unsolicited/unagented manuscripts: ☒ Yes   ☐ No
Accepts queries by: ☒ Email ☐ Fax ☐ Phone ☒ Letter
Query via email or letter. Include SASE for reply. Briefly describe the book you want to write, the intended age group, and your publishing credentials, if any. Send up to 5 pages of the mss of shorter works and 10 pages of longer works (novels). Manuscript pages will not be returned. Responds if interested.

✉ Email:
🌐 Web Site: http://www.randomhouse.com/kids

Lee & Low Books

95 Madison Avenue, New York, NY 10016
(212) 779 4400

Established:	1994	# of Employees:	–
Titles in Print:	–	Published Annually:	–

What They Publish

Publishes multicultural literature for children.

Representative Titles/Projects

- *Sweet Music in Harlem*
- *Knockin' On Wood*
- *Mama Elizabeti*

Who They Hire

Authors/Writers:
Pays royalties/advances. Buys all rights.

Editors, proofreaders, illustrators, designers, production personnel:
Rates vary. Send cover letter with current résumé.

Internships/Summer Jobs:
Internships available: ☐ Yes ☒ No   Summer Jobs Available: ☐ Yes ☒ No

How to Get Connected

Contact:
Phillip Lee, Thomas Low, Publishers
Craig Lee, Publisher, BEBOP BOOKS

Accepts unsolicited/unagented manuscripts: ☒ Yes ☐ No
Accepts queries by: ☐ Email ☐ Fax ☐ Phone ☒ Letter
Submission guidelines on website.

✉ Email:
🌐 Web Site: http://www.leeandlow.com

Lerner Publishing

241 First Avenue North, Minneapolis, MN 55401
(612) 332 3344

Established:	1959	# of Employees:	–
Titles in Print:	1000	Published Annually:	–

What They Publish

Publishes high quality children's books for the K–12 markets.

Representative Titles/Projects

- *Almost to Freedom*
- *Ronald Reagan*
- Visual Geography® Series

Who They Hire

Authors/Writers:
Pays royalties/advances. Buys all rights.

Editors, proofreaders, illustrators, designers, production personnel:
Rates vary. Send cover letter with current résumé.

Internships/Summer Jobs:
Internships available: ☐ Yes ☒ No   Summer Jobs Available: ☐ Yes ☒ No

How to Get Connected

Contact:
Mary Rodgers, Editor in Chief
Ellen Stein, Executive Editor
Marcia Marshall, Senior Editor
Jennifer Zimian, Nonfiction Editor

Accepts unsolicited/unagented manuscripts: ☒ Yes ☐ No
Accepts queries by: ☐ Email ☐ Fax ☐ Phone ☒ Letter
Query first. Responds if interested.

✉ Email: info@lernerbooks.com
🌐 Web Site: http://www.lernerbooks.com

Little Brown Children's Books

1271 Avenue of the Americas, 11th Floor, New York NY 10020

Established:	–	# of Employees:	–
Titles in Print:	–	Published Annually:	–

What They Publish

Publishes children's books.

Representative Titles/Projects

- *Saying Goodbye to Lulu*
- *She'll Be Comin' Round the Mountain*
- *Blow Out the Moon*

Who They Hire

Authors/Writers:
Pays royalties/advances. Buys all rights.

Editors, proofreaders, illustrators, designers, production personnel:
Rates vary. Send cover letter with current résumé.

Internships/Summer Jobs:
Internships available: ☒ Yes ☐ No   Summer Jobs Available: ☐ Yes ☒ No

How to Get Connected

Contact:
Megan Tingley, Editor in Chief
Andrea Spooner, Executive Editor
Cindy Eagan, Amy Hsu, Jennifer Hunt, Alvina Ling, Editors

Accepts unsolicited/unagented manuscripts: ☐ Yes ☒ No
Accepts queries by: ☐ Email ☐ Fax ☐ Phone ☐ Letter
Submission guidelines on website. Responds in 8–10 weeks.

✉ Email:
🌐 Web Site: http://www.lbchildrens.com

Little Mai Press

102 River Drive, Lake Hiawatha, NJ 07034
(973) 331 9648

Established:	1998	# of Employees:	–
Titles in Print:	–	Published Annually:	–

What They Publish

Publishes illustrated books for children and planning to expand into juvenile fiction in 2005.

Note: This publisher is not accepting submissions through 2006, but recommends that you check with them periodically as their business grows and needs change.

Representative Titles/Projects

- *Freddie Q. Freckle*
- *I've Got Mail*
- *Why Me?*

Who They Hire

Authors/Writers:
N/A

Editors, proofreaders, illustrators, designers, production personnel:
Rates vary. Send cover letter with current résumé.

Internships/Summer Jobs:
Internships available: ☐ Yes ☒ No   Summer Jobs Available: ☐ Yes ☒ No

How to Get Connected

Contact:
Robert Messinger, Publisher

Accepts unsolicited/unagented manuscripts: ☐ Yes ☒ No
Accepts queries by: ☐ Email ☐ Fax ☐ Phone ☒ Letter
Submission guidelines on website. Responds in 8–10 weeks.

✉ Email: lmaipress@aol.com
🌐 Web Site: http://www.littlemaipress.com

Little Simon

An Imprint of Simon & Schuster Children's Publishing
1230 Avenue of the Americas, New York, NY 10020

Established:	–	# of Employees:	–
Titles in Print:	–	Published Annually:	65

What They Publish

Publishes children's novelty and branded books.

Representative Titles/Projects

- *Birthday Bugs*
- *Where Is Baby's Bellybutton?*
- Matchbox Series

Who They Hire

Authors/Writers:
Pays royalties/advances. Buys all rights.

Editors, proofreaders, illustrators, designers, production personnel:
Rates vary. Send cover letter with current résumé.

Internships/Summer Jobs:
Internships available: ☒ Yes ☐ No   Summer Jobs Available: ☐ Yes ☒ No

How to Get Connected

Contact:
Robin Corey, Executive Vice President and Publisher
Cindy Alvarez, Vice President and Editorial Director

Accepts unsolicited/unagented manuscripts: ☐ Yes   ☒ No
Accepts queries by: ☐ Email ☐ Fax ☐ Phone ☒ Letter
Query only. Responds if interested.

✉ Email:
🌐 Web Site: http://www.simonsayskids.com

Magination Press

750 First Street NE, Washington, DC 20002
(800) 374 2721

Established:	1987	# of Employees:	–
Titles in Print:	–	Published Annually:	–

What They Publish

Publishes special books for children with special concerns.

Representative Titles/Projects

- *Blue Cheese Breath and Stinky Feet*
- *Rising Above the Storm Clouds*
- *Jenny Is Scared! When Sad Things Happen In The World*

Who They Hire

Authors/Writers:
Pays royalties/advances. Buys all rights.

Editors, proofreaders, illustrators, designers, production personnel:
Rates vary. Send cover letter with current résumé.

Internships/Summer Jobs:
Internships available: ☐ Yes ☒ No   Summer Jobs Available: ☐ Yes ☒ No

How to Get Connected

Contact:
Dennis Hillman, Publisher

Accepts unsolicited/unagented manuscripts: ☒ Yes   ☐ No
Accepts queries by: ☐ Email ☐ Fax ☐ Phone ☒ Letter
Query first. Responds if interested.

✉ Email: magination@apa.org
🌐 Web Site: http://www.maginationpress.com

Maupin House

PO Box 90148, Gainesville, Florida   32607
(800) 524 0634

Established:	1990	# of Employees:	–
Titles in Print:	–	Published Annually:	–

What They Publish

Publishes professional resources for K–12 teachers.

Representative Titles/Projects

- *Building a Writing Community*
- *Snipper Critters*
- *Idioms for Aliens*

Who They Hire

Authors/Writers:
Pays royalties/advances. Buys all rights.

Editors, proofreaders, illustrators, designers, production personnel:
Rates vary. Send cover letter with current résumé.

Internships/Summer Jobs:
Internships available: ☐ Yes ☒ No   Summer Jobs Available: ☐ Yes ☒ No

How to Get Connected

Contact:
Julie Graddy, Publisher

Accepts unsolicited/unagented manuscripts: ☒ Yes ☐ No
Accepts queries by: ☐ Email ☐ Fax ☐ Phone ☒ Letter
Query first. Responds if interested.

✉ Email: jgraddy@maupinhouse.com
🌐 Web Site: http://www.maupinhouse.com

McClanahan Book Company

23 West 26th Street, New York, NY 10010
(212) 725 1515

Established:	–	# of Employees:	–
Titles in Print:	–	Published Annually:	–

What They Publish

Publishes educational children's books, workbooks, activity books, and board books.

Representative Titles/Projects

- *My Big Book of Mother Goose Rhymes*
- *100 Fish & 10 Worms*
- *Puss in Boots*

Who They Hire

Authors/Writers:
Pays royalties/advances. Buys all rights.

Editors, proofreaders, illustrators, designers, production personnel:
Rates vary. Send cover letter with current résumé.

Internships/Summer Jobs:
Internships available: ☐ Yes ☒ No   Summer Jobs Available: ☐ Yes ☒ No

How to Get Connected

Contact:
Susan McClanahan, President

Accepts unsolicited/unagented manuscripts: ☒ Yes ☐ No
Accepts queries by: ☐ Email ☐ Fax ☐ Phone ☒ Letter
Query first. Responds if interested.

✉ Email:
🌐 Web Site:

Margaret K. McElderry Books

An Imprint of Simon & Schuster Children's Books
1230 Avenue of the Americas, New York, NY 10020
(212) 698 2761

Established:	1971	# of Employees:	–
Titles in Print:	100s	Published Annually:	30–35

What They Publish

Publishes origianal hardcover trade books for children pre-school through teen. They publish picture books, poetry, fantasy, middle grade fiction, and teen fiction.

Representative Titles/Projects

- *Bear Snores On,* by Karma Wilson, illustrated by Jane Chapman
- *Clovermead*, by David Randall
- *Mayday! Mayday! A Coast Guard Rescue*, by Chris L. Demarest

Who They Hire

Authors/Illustrators:
Advance and royalty.

Editors, proofreaders, illustrators, designers, production personnel:
Does not hire outside resources.

Internships/Summer Jobs:
Internships available: ☒ Yes ☐ No   Summer Jobs Available: ☐ Yes   ☒ No
Visit website for additional information about their internship program.

How to Get Connected

Contact:
Emma Dryden, Vice President and Editorial Director
Karen Wojtyla, Senior Editor

Accepts unsolicited/unagented manuscripts: ☐ Yes   ☒ No
Accepts queries by: ☐ Email ☐ Fax ☐ Phone ☒ Letter
Publisher is not currently evaluating unsolicited manuscripts. You may send a query letter along with a brief résumé of your previous publishing credits and a SASE. Writers guidelines available with SASE.

✉ Email: Do not email.
🌐 Web Site: http://www.simonsayskids.com

me+mi publishing

128 South County Farm Road, Suite E, Wheaton, IL 60187
(630) 752 9951

Established:	1992	# of Employees:	–
Titles in Print:	--	Published Annually:	–

What They Publish

Publishes Pre-K English and Spanish children's books.

Representative Titles/Projects

- *My Family*
- *Opposites*
- *Jobs Around My Neighborhood*

Who They Hire

Authors/Writers:
Pays royalties/advances. Buys all rights.

Editors, proofreaders, illustrators, designers, production personnel:
Rates vary. Send cover letter with current résumé.

Internships/Summer Jobs:
Internships available: ☐ Yes ☒ No   Summer Jobs Available: ☐ Yes ☒ No

How to Get Connected

Contact:
Gladys Rosa-Mendoza, Publisher

Accepts unsolicited/unagented manuscripts: ☐ Yes ☒ No
Accepts queries by: ☐ Email ☐ Fax ☐ Phone ☐ Letter
Submission guidelines on website. Responds in 8–10 weeks.

✉ Email: m3@memima.com
🌐 Web Site: http://www.memima.com

Meadowbrook Press

5451 Smetana Drive, Minnetonka, MN 55343
(952) 930 1100

Established:	1975	# of Employees:	–
Titles in Print:	–	Published Annually:	–

What They Publish

Publishes parenting, childcare, and humor titles, children's fiction and poetry.

Representative Titles/Projects

- *Playing for Pride*
- *Bad Case of the Giggles*
- Girls to the Rescue Series

Who They Hire

Authors/Writers:
Pays royalties/advances. Buys all rights.

Editors, proofreaders, illustrators, designers, production personnel:
Rates vary. Send cover letter with current résumé.

Internships/Summer Jobs:
Internships available: ☐ Yes ☒ No   Summer Jobs Available: ☐ Yes ☒ No

How to Get Connected

Contact:
Bruce Lansky, Publisher

Accepts unsolicited/unagented manuscripts: ☐ Yes ☒ No
Accepts queries by: ☐ Email ☐ Fax ☐ Phone ☒ Letter
Submission guidelines on website.

✉ Email: awiechmann@meadowbrookpress.com
🕭 Web Site: http://www.meadowbrookpress.com

Medallion Press, Inc.

212 Franklin Street, Suite 2, Barrington, IL 60010
(847) 756 4316

Established:	–	# of Employees:	–
Titles in Print:	–	Published Annually:	–

What They Publish

Publishes paperback fiction for young adults.

Representative Titles/Projects

- *The Secret of Shabaz*
- *Horse Passages*

Who They Hire

Authors/Writers:
Pays royalties/advances. Buys all rights.

Editors, proofreaders, illustrators, designers, production personnel:
Rates vary. Send cover letter with current résumé.

Internships/Summer Jobs:
Internships available: ☐ Yes ☒ No   Summer Jobs Available: ☐ Yes ☒ No

How to Get Connected

Contact:
Pam Ficarella, Editor in Chief
Peggy McMillan, Acquisitions Editor

Accepts unsolicited/unagented manuscripts: ☐ Yes ☒ No
Accepts queries by: ☐ Email ☐ Fax ☐ Phone ☐ Letter
Submission guidelines on website. Responds if interested.

✉ Email: pam@medallionpress.com
🌐 Web Site: http://www.medallionpress.com

Milkweed Editions

1011 Washington Avenue South, #300, Minneapolis, MN 55415
(612) 332 3192

Established: –   # of Employees: –
Titles in Print: –   Published Annually: –

What They Publish

Publishes literary books for young readers.

Representative Titles/Projects

- *Hard Times for Jake Smith*
- Stories From Where We Live Series
-

Who They Hire

Authors/Writers:
Pays royalties/advances. Buys all rights.

Editors, proofreaders, illustrators, designers, production personnel:
Rates vary. Send cover letter with current résumé.

Internships/Summer Jobs:
Internships available: ☐ Yes ☒ No   Summer Jobs Available: ☐ Yes ☒ No

How to Get Connected

Contact:
H. Emerson Blake, Editor in Chief
Laurie Bress, Managing Editor

Accepts unsolicited/unagented manuscripts: ☒ Yes ☐ No
Accepts queries by: ☐ Email ☐ Fax ☐ Phone ☒ Letter
Submission guidelines on website.

✉ Email: blake@milkweed.org
🌐 Web Site: http://www.milkweed.org

The Millbrook Press

2 Old New Milford Road, Brookfield, CT 06804
(203) 740 2220

Established:	1991	# of Employees:	–
Titles in Print:	1,000	Published Annually:	130

What They Publish

Publishes nonfiction and literature for children K–12.

Representative Titles/Projects

- *Get to Work, Truck*
- *What Are You Waiting For?*
- *The American Indian Wars*

Who They Hire

Authors/Writers:
Pays royalties/advances. Buys all rights.

Editors, proofreaders, illustrators, designers, production personnel:
Rates vary. Send cover letter with current résumé.

Internships/Summer Jobs:
Internships available: ☐ Yes ☒ No   Summer Jobs Available: ☐ Yes ☒ No

How to Get Connected

Contact:
Howard Graham, Publisher

Accepts unsolicited/unagented manuscripts: ☒ Yes ☐ No
Accepts queries by: ☐ Email ☐ Fax ☐ Phone ☐ Letter
Submission guidelines on website. Responds if interested.

✉ Email:
🌐 Web Site: http://www.millbrookpress.com

Mondo Publishing

980 Avenue of the Americas, New York, NY 10018
(212) 268 3560

Established:	–	# of Employees:	–
Titles in Print:	–	Published Annually:	–

What They Publish

Publishes literacy resources for K–5 educators.

Representative Titles/Projects

- *Animal Crackers*
- *Map the Weather*
- *Sea Cave*

Who They Hire

Authors/Writers:

Pays royalties/advances. Buys all rights.

Editors, proofreaders, illustrators, designers, production personnel:

Rates vary. Send cover letter with current résumé.

Internships/Summer Jobs:

Internships available: ☐ Yes ☒ No   Summer Jobs Available: ☐ Yes ☒ No

How to Get Connected

Contact:

Mark Vineis, Publisher

Accepts unsolicited/unagented manuscripts: ☒ Yes ☐ No
Accepts queries by: ☐ Email ☐ Fax ☐ Phone ☒ Letter
Query first. Respond if interested.

✉ Email: info@mondopub.com
🌐 Web Site: http://www.mondopub.com

Moody Publishers

820 N. LaSalle Street, Chicago, IL 60610
(312) 329 2102

Established:	1894	# of Employees:	66
Titles in Print:	700	Published Annually:	70

What They Publish

Publishes Christian literature, Bibles, Bible study aids, and nonfiction about finances from a Christian perspective for an evangelical Christian market of young people and adults.

Representative Titles/Projects

- *The Love Language of God*, by Gary Chapman
- *Unlocking the Bible Story*, by Colin Smith
- *A Place of Quiet Rest*, by Nancy Leigh DeMoss

Who They Hire

Writers:
Pays royalty/pays advances. Retains all rights.

Editors, proofreaders, indexers:
Rates vary. Send cover letter with current résumé.

Internships/Summer Jobs:
Internships available: ☒ Yes ☐ No   Summer Jobs Available: ☐ Yes ☒ No

How to Get Connected

Contact:
Greg Thornton, Vice President, Executive Editor

Accepts unsolicited/unagented manuscripts: ☒ Yes ☐ No
Accepts queries by: ☐ Email ☐ Fax ☐ Phone ☒ Letter
Send proposal with one or two sample chapters or a synopsis that describes the proposed work's theme and target audience. Do not phone, show up without an appointment, submit inappropriate ideas, or send complete manuscripts. Include return postage if you want your submission returned. Responds in 8 weeks.

✉ Email: pressinfo@moody.edu
🌐 Web Site: http://www.moodypublishers.com

NewSouth Books

105 South Court Street, Montgomery, AL 36104
(334) 834 3556

Established:	1984	# of Employees:	–
Titles in Print:	70	Published Annually:	–

What They Publish

Publishes regional books of national interest. Junebug Books is their imprint for children specializing in children's chapter books, including African American and Native American subjects.

Representative Titles/Projects

- *Shine Annie*
- *Hank Aaron: The Life of the Home Run King*
- *Johnnie Carr: A Quiet Life of Activism*

Who They Hire

Authors/Writers:
Pays royalties/advances. Buys all rights.

Editors, proofreaders, illustrators, designers, production personnel:
Rates vary. Send cover letter with current résumé.

Internships/Summer Jobs:
Internships available: ☐ Yes ☒ No   Summer Jobs Available: ☐ Yes ☒ No

How to Get Connected

Contact:
Suzanne La Rosa, Publisher
Randall Williams, Editor in Chief, Junebug Books

Accepts unsolicited/unagented manuscripts: ☒ Yes ☐ No
Accepts queries by: ☐ Email ☐ Fax ☐ Phone ☒ Letter
Submission guidelines on website. Query first.

✉ Email: randall@newsouthbooks.com
🌐 Web Site: http://www.newsouthbooks.com

North-South Books

875 Sixth Avenue, Suite 1901, New York, NY 10001
(212) 706 4545

Established:	1961	# of Employees:	–
Titles in Print:	–	Published Annually:	–

What They Publish

Publishes books that forge links between readers of all ages around the world.

Representative Titles/Projects

- *The Rainbow Fish*
- *Andrew's Angry Words*
- *Lord of the Cranes*

Who They Hire

Authors/Writers:
Pays royalties/advances. Buys all rights.

Editors, proofreaders, illustrators, designers, production personnel:
Rates vary. Send cover letter with current résumé.

Internships/Summer Jobs:
Internships available: ☐ Yes ☒ No   Summer Jobs Available: ☐ Yes ☒ No

How to Get Connected

Contact:
Mary-Alice Moore, Editor in Chief

Accepts unsolicited/unagented manuscripts: ☐ Yes   ☐ No
Accepts queries by: ☐ Email ☐ Fax ☐ Phone ☐ Letter
Submission guidelines on website.

✉ Email:
🌐 Web Site: http://www.northsouth.com

Novello Festival Press

310 N Tryon Street, Charlotte, NC 28202
(704) 432 0153

Established:	–	# of Employees:	–
Titles in Print:	–	Published Annually:	–

What They Publish

This publisher is the country's only library-sponsored publisher. They publish literary fiction, nonfiction, poetry, and children's literature.

Representative Titles/Projects

- *Leaving Maggie Hope*
- *Jasper*
- *Hungry for Home*

Who They Hire

Authors/Writers:
Pays royalties/advances. Buys all rights.

Editors, proofreaders, illustrators, designers, production personnel:
Rates vary. Send cover letter with current résumé.

Internships/Summer Jobs:
Internships available: ☐ Yes ☒ No   Summer Jobs Available: ☐ Yes ☒ No

How to Get Connected

Contact:
Frye Gaillard, Executive Editor

Accepts unsolicited/unagented manuscripts: ☒ Yes   ☐ No
Accepts queries by: ☐ Email ☐ Fax ☐ Phone ☒ Letter
Submission guidelines on website. Responds if interested.

✉ Email: fryegaillard@aol.com
🌐 Web Site: http://www.novellopress.org

The Oliver Press

5707 West 36th Street, Minneapolis, MN 55416-2510
(952) 926 8981

Established:	–	# of Employees:	–
Titles in Print:	–	Published Annually:	–

What They Publish

Publishes history, biography, and science books for young readers.

Representative Titles/Projects

- *America's Most Influential First Ladies*
- *You Are the Explorer*
- *Construction: Building the Impossible*

Who They Hire

Authors/Writers:
Pays royalties/advances. Buys all rights.

Editors, proofreaders, illustrators, designers, production personnel:
Rates vary. Send cover letter with current résumé.

Internships/Summer Jobs:
Internships available: ☐ Yes ☒ No   Summer Jobs Available: ☐ Yes ☒ No

How to Get Connected

Contact:
Denise Sterling, Editor

Accepts unsolicited/unagented manuscripts: ☐ Yes   ☐ No
Accepts queries by: ☐ Email ☐ Fax ☐ Phone ☒ Letter
Submission guidelines on website.

✉ Email: queries@oliverpress.com
🌎 Web Site: http://www.oliverpress.com

Open Hand Publishing

PO Box 20207, Greensboro, NC 27420
(336) 292 8585

Established:	1981	# of Employees:	–
Titles in Print:	–	Published Annually:	–

What They Publish

Publishes multicultural juvenile literature and children's fiction.

Representative Titles/Projects

- *Squizzy the Black Squirrel*
- *Imperial Washington*
- *Juneteenth: A Celebration of Freedom*

Who They Hire

Authors/Writers:
Pays royalties/advances. Buys all rights.

Editors, proofreaders, illustrators, designers, production personnel:
Rates vary. Send cover letter with current résumé.

Internships/Summer Jobs:
Internships available: ☐ Yes ☒ No   Summer Jobs Available: ☐ Yes ☒ No

How to Get Connected

Contact:
Richard Koritz, Publisher
Sandra Koritz, Editor

Accepts unsolicited/unagented manuscripts: ☒ Yes   ☐ No
Accepts queries by: ☐ Email ☐ Fax ☐ Phone ☒ Letter
Query first. Responds if interested.

✉ Email: info@openhand.com
🌐 Web Site: http://www.openhand.com

Orca Book Publishers

PO Box 468, Custer, WA 98240
(800) 210 5277

Established:	–	# of Employees:	–
Titles in Print:	–	Published Annually:	–

What They Publish

Publishes children's books and juvenile/teen fiction.

Representative Titles/Projects

- *Blue Moon*
- *Overdrive*
- *Kicked Out*

Who They Hire

Authors/Writers:
Pays royalties/advances. Buys all rights.

Editors, proofreaders, illustrators, designers, production personnel:
Rates vary. Send cover letter with current résumé.

Internships/Summer Jobs:
Internships available: ☐ Yes ☒ No   Summer Jobs Available: ☐ Yes ☒ No

How to Get Connected

Contact:
Andrew Wooldridge; US Editor

Accepts unsolicited/unagented manuscripts: ☐ Yes   ☐ No
Accepts queries by: ☐ Email ☐ Fax ☐ Phone ☒ Letter
Submission guidelines on website. Responds if interested.

✉ Email: orca@orcabook.com
🌐 Web Site: http://www.orcabook.com

Owl Books

An Imprint of Henry Holt Books for Young Readers
115 West 18th Street, New York, NY 10011
(212) 886 9332

Established:	–	# of Employees:	–
Titles in Print:	–	Published Annually:	–

What They Publish

Publishes paperback nonfiction on parenting topics.

Representative Titles/Projects

- *The ADD Nutrition Solution: A Drug-Free 30 Day Plan*
- *Beyond Sibling Rivalry: How to Help Your Children Become Cooperative, Caring, and Compassionate*
- *Real Boys: Rescuing Our Sons From the Myths of Boyhood*

Who They Hire

Authors/Writers:
Pays royalties/advances. Buys all rights.

Editors, proofreaders, illustrators, designers, production personnel:
Rates vary. Send cover letter with current résumé.

Internships/Summer Jobs:
Internships available: ☒ Yes ☐ No   Summer Jobs Available: ☐ Yes ☒ No

How to Get Connected

Contact:
Editorial Department

Accepts unsolicited/unagented manuscripts: ☐ Yes ☒ No
Accepts queries by: ☐ Email ☐ Fax ☐ Phone ☒ Letter
Query only. Responds if interested.

✉ Email:
🌐 Web Site: http://www.henryholt.com

Parenting Press

PO Box 75267, Seattle, WA 98175
(206) 364 2900

Established:	1979	# of Employees:	–
Titles in Print:	–	Published Annually:	–

What They Publish

Publishes books for children and those who care for them.

Representative Titles/Projects

- *Without Spanking or Spoiling: A Practical Approach to Toddler and Preschool Guidance*
- *The Way I Feel*
- *Dealing With Disappointment: Helping Kids Cope When Things Don't Go Their Way*

Who They Hire

Authors/Writers:
Pays royalties/advances. Buys all rights.

Editors, proofreaders, illustrators, designers, production personnel:
Rates vary. Send cover letter with current résumé.

Internships/Summer Jobs:
Internships available: ☐ Yes ☒ No   Summer Jobs Available: ☐ Yes ☒ No

How to Get Connected

Contact:
Elizabeth Crary, Publisher

Accepts unsolicited/unagented manuscripts: ☒ Yes   ☐ No
Accepts queries by: ☐ Email ☐ Fax ☐ Phone ☒ Letter
Query first. Responds if interested.

✉ Email: fcrary@parentingpress.com
🌐 Web Site: http://www.parentingpress.com

Parklane Publishing

888 Veterans Memorial Highway, Suite 540, Hauppauge, NY 11788
(631) 234 9210

Established:	2002	# of Employees:	–
Titles in Print:	60	Published Annually:	19

What They Publish

Publishes children's books.

Representative Titles/Projects

- *Moonbeam Bear*
- *Felix and the Flying Suitcase Adventure*
- *Rip Squeak and His Friends*

Who They Hire

Authors/Writers:
Pays royalties/advances. Buys all rights.

Editors, proofreaders, illustrators, designers, production personnel:
Rates vary. Send cover letter with current résumé.

Internships/Summer Jobs:
Internships available: ☐ Yes ☒ No   Summer Jobs Available: ☐ Yes ☒ No

How to Get Connected

Contact:
Philip Rodgers, Publisher

Accepts unsolicited/unagented manuscripts: ☒ Yes   ☐ No
Accepts queries by: ☐ Email ☐ Fax ☐ Phone ☒ Letter
Query first. Responds if interested.

✉ Email: info@parklanepublishing.com
🌐 Web Site: http://www.parklanepublishing.com

Peachtree Publishers Ltd.

1700 Chattahoochee Avenue, Atlanta, GA 30318-2112
(404) 876 8761

Established:	1979	# of Employees:	–
Titles in Print:	–	Published Annually:	20

What They Publish

Publishes a variety of children's, teen's, and parenting titles.

Representative Titles/Projects

- *The Library Dragon*
- *Who Has a Belly Button*
- *Larabee*

Who They Hire

Authors/Writers:
Pays royalties/advances. Buys all rights.

Editors, proofreaders, illustrators, designers, production personnel:
Rates vary. Send cover letter with current résumé.

Internships/Summer Jobs:
Internships available: ☐ Yes ☒ No   Summer Jobs Available: ☐ Yes ☒ No

How to Get Connected

Contact:
Lisa Banim, Acquisitions Editor
Helen Harriss, Submissions Editor

Accepts unsolicited/unagented manuscripts: ☒ Yes ☐ No
Accepts queries by: ☐ Email ☐ Fax ☐ Phone ☒ Letter
Submission guidelines on website.

✉ Email: hello@peachtree-online.com
🌐 Web Site: http://www.peachtree-online.com

Pelican Publishing

PO Box 3110, Gretna, LA 70054
(800) 843 1724

Established:	1970	# of Employees:	–
Titles in Print:	500	Published Annually:	50–60

What They Publish

Publishes children's books.

This publisher is currently looking for proposals for books on topics similar to those they currently have in print.

Representative Titles/Projects

- *D.J. and the Debutante Ball*
- *A Fish Out of Water*
- *Evangeline and the Acadians*

Who They Hire

Authors/Writers:
Pays royalties/advances. Buys all rights.

Editors, proofreaders, illustrators, designers, production personnel:
Rates vary. Send cover letter with current résumé.

Internships/Summer Jobs:
Internships available: ☐ Yes ☒ No   Summer Jobs Available: ☐ Yes ☒ No

How to Get Connected

Contact:
Nancy Calhoun, Vice President

Accepts unsolicited/unagented manuscripts: ☒ Yes   ☐ No
Accepts queries by: ☐ Email ☐ Fax ☐ Phone ☒ Letter
Submission guidelines on website.

✉ Email:
🌐 Web Site: http://www.pelicanpub.com

Philomel

An Imprint of Penguin Putnam
375 Hudson Street, New York, NY 10014
(212) 366 2000

Established:	1980	# of Employees:	–
Titles in Print:	–	Published Annually:	–

What They Publish

Publishes books that inspire a global love of learning.

Representative Titles/Projects

- *The Very Hungry Caterpillar*
- *Seven Blind Mice*
- *The Ghost in the Tokaido Inn*

Who They Hire

Authors/Writers:
Pays royalties/advances. Buys all rights.

Editors, proofreaders, illustrators, designers, production personnel:
Rates vary. Send cover letter with current résumé.

Internships/Summer Jobs:
Internships available: ☒ Yes ☐ No   Summer Jobs Available: ☐ Yes ☒ No

How to Get Connected

Contact:
Michael Green, Publisher and Editorial Director
Patricia Lee Gauch, Vice President and Editor at Large

Accepts unsolicited/unagented manuscripts: ☐ Yes   ☒ No
Accepts queries by: ☐ Email ☐ Fax ☐ Phone ☒ Letter
Query only. Responds if interested.

✉ Email:
🌐 Web Site: http://www.penguinputnam.com

Picture Me Books

An Imprint of Playhouse Publishing
1566 Akron-Peninsula Road, Akron, OH 44313
(330) 762 6800

Established:	–	# of Employees:	–
Titles in Print:	–	Published Annually:	–

What They Publish

Publishes books combining children's photos into a variety of stories and themes.

Representative Titles/Projects

- Little Lucy and Friends books
- Nibble Me books
- Picture and Press books

Who They Hire

Authors/Writers:
Pays royalties/advances. Buys all rights.

Editors, proofreaders, illustrators, designers, production personnel:
Rates vary. Send cover letter with current résumé.

Internships/Summer Jobs:
Internships available: ☐ Yes ☒ No   Summer Jobs Available: ☐ Yes ☒ No

How to Get Connected

Contact:
Deborah B. D'Andrea, Editor

Accepts unsolicited/unagented manuscripts: ☐ Yes ☒ No
Accepts queries by: ☐ Email ☐ Fax ☐ Phone ☒ Letter
Query only with book ideas. Responds if interested.

✉ Email: info@playhousepublishing.com
🌐 Web Site: http://www.playhousepublishing.com

Picture Window Books

7825 Telegraph Road, Minneapolis, MN 55438
(952) 933 7182

Established:	1973	# of Employees:	42
Titles in Print:	350	Published Annually:	–

What They Publish

Publishes picture books designed to spark a child's natural love of learning.

Representative Titles/Projects

- *I Can Do It!*
- *No Fair!*
- *We Live Here Too!*

Who They Hire

Authors/Writers:
Pays royalties/advances. Buys all rights.

Editors, proofreaders, illustrators, designers, production personnel:
Rates vary. Send cover letter with current résumé.

Internships/Summer Jobs:
Internships available: ☐ Yes ☒ No   Summer Jobs Available: ☐ Yes ☒ No

How to Get Connected

Contact:
Editor

Accepts unsolicited/unagented manuscripts: ☐ Yes   ☐ No
Accepts queries by: ☐ Email ☐ Fax ☐ Phone ☒ Letter
Submission guidelines on website.

✉ Email:
🌐 Web Site: http://www.picturewindowbooks.com

Piñata Press

An Imprint of Arte Público Press
University of Houston / 425 Cullen Performance Hall, Houston, TX 77204
(713) 743 2999

Established:	1994	# of Employees:	–
Titles in Print:	–	Published Annually:	10

What They Publish

Publishes English, Spanish, and bilingual children's books written by US Hispanic authors.

Representative Titles/Projects

- *Remembering Grandma*
- *Chiles for Benito*
- *Family, Familia*

Who They Hire

Authors/Writers:
Pays royalties/advances. Buys all rights.

Editors, proofreaders, illustrators, designers, production personnel:
Rates vary. Send cover letter with current résumé.

Internships/Summer Jobs:
Internships available: ☐ Yes ☒ No   Summer Jobs Available: ☐ Yes ☒ No

How to Get Connected

Contact:
Submissions Editor

Accepts unsolicited/unagented manuscripts: ☒ Yes ☐ No
Accepts queries by: ☐ Email ☐ Fax ☐ Phone ☒ Letter
Submission guidelines on website. Responds in 2–6 months.

✉ Email:
🌐 Web Site: http://www.artepublicopress.com

Pleasant Company Publications

PO Box 620991, Middleton, WI 53562
(800) 233 0264

Established:	1986	# of Employees:	–
Titles in Print:	–	Published Annually:	–

What They Publish

Publishes books for girls that build self-esteem and reinforce positive social and moral values.

Representative Titles/Projects

- *What a Girl Loves: Puzzle Book*
- *The Big Book of Help!*
- *Angelina's Dance of Friendship*

Who They Hire

Authors/Writers:
Pays royalties/advances. Buys all rights.

Editors, proofreaders, illustrators, designers, production personnel:
Rates vary. Send cover letter with current résumé.

Internships/Summer Jobs:
Internships available: ☒ Yes ☐ No   Summer Jobs Available: ☐ Yes ☒ No

How to Get Connected

Contact:
Jodi Evert, Editorial Director

Accepts unsolicited/unagented manuscripts: ☐ Yes   ☒ No
Accepts queries by: ☐ Email ☐ Fax ☐ Phone ☒ Letter
Query only. Responds if interested.

✉ Email:
🌐 Web Site: http://www.pleasantcopublications.com

Polychrome Publishing Corporation

4509 N. Francisco Avenue, Chicago, IL 60625
(773) 478 4455

Established:	1990	# of Employees:	2
Titles in Print:	16	Published Annually:	4

What They Publish

Publishes multicultural fiction and nonfiction (with an emphasis on Asian American themes) for children; some nonfiction directed at parents as teaching aids.

Representative Titles/Projects

- *Striking It Rich*, by Debbie Leung Yamada
- *Children of Asian America*
- *Almond Cookies & Dragon Well Tea*, by Cynthia Chin Lee

Who They Hire

Writers:
Pays nominal fee, then royalty rate/pays advances. Retains all rights.

Proofreaders, illustrators, designers, indexers, production personnel:
Rates vary. Send cover letter with current résumé.

Internships/Summer Jobs:
Internships available: ☐ Yes ☒ No   Summer Jobs Available: ☐ Yes ☒ No

How to Get Connected

Contact:
Sandra Yamate

Accepts unsolicited/unagented manuscripts: ☒ Yes   ☐ No
Accepts queries by: ☐ Email ☐ Fax ☐ Phone ☒ Letter
Send query letter and/or complete manuscript. Stories and plots must have authenticity with the cultures they describe. Do not send fables, folk tales, or animated animal stories. Replies within 6–8 months.

✉ Email: polypub@earthlink.net
🌐 Web Site: http://www.polychromebooks.com

Puffin

375 Hudson Street, New York, NY 10014
(212) 366 2000

Established:	1941	# of Employees:	–
Titles in Print:	–	Published Annually:	225

What They Publish

Publishes classic children's fiction and the best new literature.

Representative Titles/Projects

- *Which Witch*
- *Madeline*
- *26 Fairmont Avenue*

Who They Hire

Authors/Writers:
Pays royalties/advances. Buys all rights.

Editors, proofreaders, illustrators, designers, production personnel:
Rates vary. Send cover letter with current résumé.

Internships/Summer Jobs:
Internships available: ☐ Yes ☒ No   Summer Jobs Available: ☐ Yes ☒ No

How to Get Connected

Contact:
Tracy Tang, Editor

Accepts unsolicited/unagented manuscripts: ☐ Yes ☒ No
Accepts queries by: ☐ Email ☐ Fax ☐ Phone ☒ Letter
Query only. Responds if interested.

✉ Email:
🌐 Web Site: http://www.penguinputnam.com

Quail Ridge Press

PO Box 123, Brandon, MI 39043
(800) 343 1583

Established:	1978	# of Employees:	–
Titles in Print:	–	Published Annually:	–

What They Publish

Publishes cookbooks, the Mississippi mystery series, and some children's books.

Representative Titles/Projects

- *Cat Hymns*
- *Hooray for Mississippi*
- *The Turtle Saver*

Who They Hire

Authors/Writers:
Pays royalties/advances. Buys all rights.

Editors, proofreaders, illustrators, designers, production personnel:
Rates vary. Send cover letter with current résumé.

Internships/Summer Jobs:
Internships available: ☐ Yes ☒ No   Summer Jobs Available: ☐ Yes ☒ No

How to Get Connected

Contact:
Barney McKee, Publisher
Gwen McKee, Editor in Chief

Accepts unsolicited/unagented manuscripts: ☒ Yes ☐ No
Accepts queries by: ☐ Email ☐ Fax ☐ Phone ☒ Letter
Query first. Responds if interested.

✉ Email: gmckee@quailridge.com
🌐 Web Site: http://www.quailridge.com

Rand McNally

P.O. Box 7600, Chicago, IL 60680
(847) 329 8100

Established:	1865	# of Employees:	–
Titles in Print:	70	Published Annually:	30

What They Publish

Publishes road atlases and maps; mileage and routing publications; educational maps; children's maps, atlases, and books; electronic multimedia products.

Representative Titles/Projects

- *2003 Road Atlas Large Scale*
- *StreetFinder and TripMaker Deluxe* (software)
- *Children's Atlas of the World*

Who They Hire

Writers:
Pays fees upon acceptance. Retains all rights.

Editors, proofreaders, illustrators, designers, indexers, production personnel:
Rates vary. Send cover letter with current résumé.

Internships/Summer Jobs:
Internships available: ☒ Yes ☐ No   Summer Jobs Available: ☐ Yes ☒ No

How to Get Connected

Laurie Borman, Editorial Director

Accepts unsolicited/unagented manuscripts: ☐ Yes ☒ No
Accepts queries by: ☐ Email ☐ Fax ☐ Phone ☒ Letter
Do not send unsolicited manuscripts. Prospective authors should send an SASE with their queries. Responds in 8–10 weeks.

✉ Email: n/a
🌐 Web Site: http://www.randmcnally.com

Random House Children's Books

1745 Broadway, New York, NY 10019
(212) 782 9000

Established:	–	# of Employees:	–
Titles in Print:	–	Published Annually:	100s

What They Publish

Publishes children's books.

Representative Titles/Projects

- *Pinky Dinky Doo*
- Junie B. Jones Series
- *Read-Aloud Rhymes*

Who They Hire

Authors/Writers:
Pays royalties/advances. Buys all rights.

Illustrators:
Rates vary. Send cover letter with current résumé and samples.

Internships/Summer Jobs:
Internships available: ☒ Yes ☐ No   Summer Jobs Available: ☐ Yes ☒ No

How to Get Connected

Contact:
Heidi Kilgras, Mallory Loehr, Editors

Accepts unsolicited/unagented manuscripts: ☐ Yes ☒ No
Accepts queries by: ☐ Email ☐ Fax ☐ Phone ☒ Letter
Query only. Responds if interested.

✉ Email:
🌐 Web Site: http://www.randomhouse.com/kids

Raven Tree Press

200 S Washington Street, Suite 306, Green Bay, WI 54301
(920) 438 1605

Established:	2000	# of Employees:	–
Titles in Print:	–	Published Annually:	–

What They Publish

Publishes bilingual picture books for children.

Representative Titles/Projects

- *Even More / Todavia Más*
- *Yelly Kelly / Kelly, el Gritón*
- *Oh, Crumps! / ¡Ay, Caramba!*

Who They Hire

Authors/Writers:
Pays royalties/advances. Buys all rights.

Editors, proofreaders, illustrators, designers, production personnel:
Rates vary. Send cover letter with current résumé.

Internships/Summer Jobs:
Internships available: ☐ Yes ☒ No   Summer Jobs Available: ☐ Yes ☒ No

How to Get Connected

Contact:
Editor

Accepts unsolicited/unagented manuscripts: ☐ Yes   ☐ No
Accepts queries by: ☐ Email ☐ Fax ☐ Phone ☒ Letter
Submission guidelines on website.

✉ Email: raven@raventreepress.com
🌐 Web Site: http://www.raventreepress.com

Redleaf Press

10 Yorktown Court, St. Paul, MN 55117
(800) 423 8309

Established:	1973	# of Employees:	–
Titles in Print:	90	Published Annually:	12–15

What They Publish

Publishes early childhood and childcare books.

Representative Titles/Projects

- *Good Going*
- *Designs for Living and Learning*
- *No Biting*

Who They Hire

Authors/Writers:
Pays royalties/advances. Buys all rights.

Editors, proofreaders, illustrators, designers, production personnel:
Rates vary. Send cover letter with current résumé.

Internships/Summer Jobs:
Internships available: ☐ Yes ☒ No   Summer Jobs Available: ☐ Yes ☒ No

How to Get Connected

Contact:
Eileen Nelson, Director
Kathy Kolb, Editor in Chief
Beth Wallace, Acquisitions Editor

Accepts unsolicited/unagented manuscripts: ☐ Yes ☐ No
Accepts queries by: ☐ Email ☐ Fax ☐ Phone ☒ Letter
Submission guidelines on website.

✉ Email: Wallace@redleafpress.org
🌐 Web Site: http://www.redleafpress.org

Rising Moon

An Imprint of Northland Publishing
PO Box 1389, Flagstaff, AZ 86001
(928) 774 5251

Established:	1988	# of Employees:	–
Titles in Print:	–	Published Annually:	–

What They Publish

Publishes illustrated children's books.

Representative Titles/Projects

- *Do Princesses Wear Hiking Boots?*
- *I Howl I Growl*
- *Farmer McPeepers and His Missing Milk Cows*

Who They Hire

Authors/Writers:

Pays royalties/advances. Buys all rights.

Editors, proofreaders, illustrators, designers, production personnel:

Rates vary. Send cover letter with current résumé.

Internships/Summer Jobs:

Internships available: ☐ Yes ☒ No   Summer Jobs Available: ☐ Yes ☒ No

How to Get Connected

Contact:

Theresa Howell, Rebecca Gomez, Children's Book Editors

Accepts unsolicited/unagented manuscripts: ☐ Yes ☐ No
Accepts queries by: ☐ Email ☐ Fax ☐ Phone ☒ Letter
Submission guidelines on website.

✉ Email: editorial@northlandpub.com
🌐 Web Site: http://www.northlandpub.com

Roaring Brook Press

A Division of Holtzbrinck Publishing Holdings Limited Partnership
143 West Street, New Milford, CT 06776
(203) 740 2220

Established:	2001	# of Employees:	6
Titles in Print:	80	Published Annually:	35–40

What They Publish

Publishes fiction and nonfiction titles and picture books for children and teens.

Representative Titles/Projects

- *The Man Who Walked Between the Towers* (2004 Caldecott)
- *My Friend Rabbit* (2003 Caldecott)
-

Who They Hire

Authors/Writers:
Pays royalties/advances. Buys all rights.

Editors, proofreaders, illustrators, designers, production personnel:
Rates vary.

Internships/Summer Jobs:
Internships available: ☐ Yes ☒ No   Summer Jobs Available: ☐ Yes ☒ No

How to Get Connected

Contact:
 Deborah Brodie, Neal Porter, Editors

Accepts unsolicited/unagented manuscripts: ☐ Yes ☒ No
Accepts queries by: ☐ Email ☐ Fax ☐ Phone ☐ Letter
Works solely with literary agents.

✉ Email:
🌐 Web Site:

Robbie Dean Press

2910 East Eisenhower Parkway, Ann Arbor, MI 48108
(734) 973 9511

Established:	–	# of Employees:	–
Titles in Print:	–	Published Annually:	–

What They Publish

Publishes children's books, educational texts, and an international journal for English teachers.

Representative Titles/Projects

- *The Children's Computer Handbook: Just Follow the Bug*
- *Soar With the Angels: a Children's Book*
- *Reesy: A Little Girl Learning Life's Lessons*

Who They Hire

Authors/Writers:
Pays royalties/advances. Buys all rights.

Editors, proofreaders, illustrators, designers, production personnel:
Rates vary. Send cover letter with current résumé.

Internships/Summer Jobs:
Internships available: ☐ Yes ☒ No   Summer Jobs Available: ☐ Yes ☒ No

How to Get Connected

Contact:
Fairy C. Hayes-Scott, PhD, Publisher

Accepts unsolicited/unagented manuscripts: ☒ Yes ☐ No
Accepts queries by: ☐ Email ☐ Fax ☐ Phone ☒ Letter
Query first. Responds if interested.

✉ Email: fairyha@aol.com
🌐 Web Site: http://www.robbiedeanpress.com

The Rosen Publishing Group

29 East 21st Street, New York, NY 10010
(212) 777 3017

Established:	1950	# of Employees:	–
Titles in Print:	–	Published Annually:	225

What They Publish

Publishes quality non-fiction for Pre-K through high school in all subject areas.

Representative Titles/Projects

- *A Historical Atlas of Jordan*
- *Junior High Journalism*
- *The Library of Future Medicine*

Who They Hire

Authors/Writers:
Pays royalties/advances. Buys all rights.

Editors, proofreaders, illustrators, designers, production personnel:
Rates vary. Send cover letter with current résumé.

Internships/Summer Jobs:
Internships available: ☐ Yes ☒ No   Summer Jobs Available: ☐ Yes ☒ No

How to Get Connected

Contact:
Roger Rosen, President

Accepts unsolicited/unagented manuscripts: ☒ Yes   ☐ No
Accepts queries by: ☐ Email ☐ Fax ☐ Phone ☒ Letter
Query first. Responds if interested.

✉ Email: info@rosenpub.com
🌐 Web Site: http://www.rosenpublishing.com

Royal Fireworks Press

First Avenue, Unionville, NY 10988
(845) 726 4444

Established:	1979	# of Employees:	–
Titles in Print:	–	Published Annually:	–

What They Publish

Publishes teen novels, young adult coming-of-age novels, and materials for gifted education grades K–12.

Representative Titles/Projects

- *Grammar Town*
- *Boys Should Be Boys*
- *Bully Frog*

Who They Hire

Authors/Writers:
Pays royalties/advances. Buys all rights.

Editors, proofreaders, illustrators, designers, production personnel:
Rates vary. Send cover letter with current résumé.

Internships/Summer Jobs:
Internships available: ☐ Yes ☒ No   Summer Jobs Available: ☐ Yes ☒ No

How to Get Connected

Contact:
Dr. T.M. Kemnitz, CEO

Accepts unsolicited/unagented manuscripts: ☒ Yes   ☐ No
Accepts queries by: ☒ Email ☐ Fax ☐ Phone ☒ Letter
Query first. Responds if interested.

✉ Email: mail@rfwp.com
🌐 Web Site: http://www.rfwp.com

Running Press Kids

125 South 22nd Street, Philadelphia, PA 19103
(215) 567 5080

Established:	–	# of Employees:	–
Titles in Print:	–	Published Annually:	–

What They Publish

Publishes children's books.

Representative Titles/Projects

- *The Thread of Life*
- *Lift the Lid on Mummies*
- *Numbers*

Who They Hire

Authors/Writers:
Pays royalties/advances. Buys all rights.

Editors, proofreaders, illustrators, designers, production personnel:
Rates vary. Send cover letter with current résumé.

Internships/Summer Jobs:
Internships available: ☐ Yes ☒ No   Summer Jobs Available: ☐ Yes ☒ No

How to Get Connected

Contact:
Andra Serlin, Elizabeth Shiflett, Editors

Accepts unsolicited/unagented manuscripts: ☐ Yes   ☐ No
Accepts queries by: ☐ Email ☐ Fax ☐ Phone ☒ Letter
Submission guidelines on website.

✉ Email:
🌐 Web Site: http://www.runningpress.com

Scholastic Press

557 Broadway, New York, NY 10012
(212) 343 6100

Established:	1921	# of Employees:	10,000
Titles in Print:	–	Published Annually:	–

What They Publish

Publishes books and materials that educate, entertain, and motivate children grades K–12.

Representative Titles/Projects

- *All About My Body*
- *Look Up to the Sky*
- *Snacks Rule!*

Who They Hire

Authors/Writers:
Pays royalties/advances. Buys all rights.

Editors, proofreaders, illustrators, designers, production personnel:
Rates vary. Send cover letter with current résumé.

Internships/Summer Jobs:
Internships available: ☒ Yes ☐ No   Summer Jobs Available: ☐ Yes ☒ No

How to Get Connected

Contact:
Barbara A. Marcus, President, Children's Book Publishing
Amy Griffin, David Levithan, Tracy Mack, Liz Szabla, Lauren Thompson, Uitgeverij Vassallucci, Craig Walker, Ken Wright, Editors

Accepts unsolicited/unagented manuscripts: ☒ Yes   ☐ No
Accepts queries by: ☐ Email ☐ Fax ☐ Phone ☒ Letter
Query first with ideas and credentials. Responds if interested.

✉ Email:
🌐 Web Site: http://www.scholastic.com

School Zone Publishing

PO Box 777, Grand Haven, MI 49417
(616) 846 5030

Established:	–	# of Employees:	100
Titles in Print:	–	Published Annually:	–

What They Publish

Publishes educational material for children in preschool through sixth grade.

Representative Titles/Projects

- *Alphabet K–1*
- *Spelling Puzzles 2*
- *Math Basics 5–6*

Who They Hire

Authors/Writers:

Pays royalties/advances. Buys all rights.

Editors, proofreaders, illustrators, designers, production personnel:

Rates vary. Send cover letter with current résumé.

Internships/Summer Jobs:

Internships available: ☐ Yes ☒ No   Summer Jobs Available: ☐ Yes ☒ No

How to Get Connected

Contact:

Lisa Carmona, Executive Editor

Accepts unsolicited/unagented manuscripts: ☒ Yes   ☐ No
Accepts queries by: ☐ Email ☐ Fax ☐ Phone ☒ Letter
Query first. Responds if interested.

✉ Email:
🌐 Web Site: http://www.schoolzone.com

Silver Dolphin Books

An Imprint of Advantage Press
5880 Oberlin Drive, San Diego, CA 92121
(858) 457 2500

Established:	–	# of Employees:	–
Titles in Print:	–	Published Annually:	–

What They Publish

Publishes interactive novelty and educational books for children Pre-K through 12-year-olds.

Representative Titles/Projects

- *Uncover a Shark*
- *Totally Aliens*
- *Totally Bugs*

Who They Hire

Authors/Writers:
Pays royalties/advances. Buys all rights.

Editors, proofreaders, illustrators, designers, production personnel:
Rates vary. Send cover letter with current résumé.

Internships/Summer Jobs:
Internships available: ☐ Yes ☒ No   Summer Jobs Available: ☐ Yes ☒ No

How to Get Connected

Contact:
Lilian Shia Nordland, Associate Publisher

Accepts unsolicited/unagented manuscripts: ☒ Yes ☐ No
Accepts queries by: ☐ Email ☐ Fax ☐ Phone ☒ Letter
Query first. Responds if interested.

✉ Email:
🌐 Web Site: http://www.advantagebooksonline.com

Simon & Schuster Children's Books

1230 Avenue of the Americas, New York, NY 10020.

Established:	–	# of Employees:	–
Titles in Print:	–	Published Annually:	–

What They Publish

Publishes children's books for all ages.

Representative Titles/Projects

- *Birthday Bugs*
- Eloise Series
- Nancy Drew Girl Detective Series

Who They Hire

Authors/Writers:
Pays royalties/advances. Buys all rights.

Editors, proofreaders, illustrators, designers, production personnel:
Rates vary. Send cover letter with current résumé.

Internships/Summer Jobs:
Internships available: ☒ Yes ☐ No   Summer Jobs Available: ☐ Yes ☒ No

How to Get Connected

Contact:
David Gale, Editorial Director
Brenda Bowen, Jennifer Klonsky, Editors

Accepts unsolicited/unagented manuscripts: ☐ Yes ☒ No
Accepts queries by: ☐ Email ☐ Fax ☐ Phone ☒ Letter
Query only. Responds if interested.

✉ Email:
🌐 Web Site: http://www.simonsayskids.com

Simon Pulse

1230 Avenue of the Americas, New York, NY 10020

Established:	–	# of Employees:	–
Titles in Print:	–	Published Annually:	–

What They Publish

Publishes teen paperback books.

Representative Titles/Projects

- *Confessions of a Backup Dancer*
- *Don't Cramp My Style*
- *Things Get Hectic*

Who They Hire

Authors/Writers:
Pays royalties/advances. Buys all rights.

Editors, proofreaders, illustrators, designers, production personnel:
Rates vary. Send cover letter with current résumé.

Internships/Summer Jobs:
Internships available: ☒ Yes ☐ No   Summer Jobs Available: ☐ Yes ☒ No

How to Get Connected

Contact:
Bethany Buck, Editorial Director
Julia Richardson, Editor

Accepts unsolicited/unagented manuscripts: ☐ Yes ☒ No
Accepts queries by: ☐ Email ☐ Fax ☐ Phone ☒ Letter
Query only. Responds if interested.

✉ Email:
🌐 Web Site: http://www.simonsayskids.com

Sleeping Bear Press

310 N Main Street, #300, Chelsea, MI 48118
(734) 475 4411

Established:	–	# of Employees:	–
Titles in Print:	–	Published Annually:	–

What They Publish

Publishes a variety of books for children of all ages.

Representative Titles/Projects

- *Buzzy the Bumblebee*
- *The Legend of Lee Lanau*
- *Winter's Gift*

Who They Hire

Authors/Writers:
Pays royalties/advances. Buys all rights.

Editors, proofreaders, illustrators, designers, production personnel:
Rates vary. Send cover letter with current résumé.

Internships/Summer Jobs:
Internships available: ☐ Yes ☒ No   Summer Jobs Available: ☐ Yes ☒ No

How to Get Connected

Contact:
Heather Hughes, Executive Editor

Accepts unsolicited/unagented manuscripts: ☒ Yes   ☐ No
Accepts queries by: ☐ Email ☐ Fax ☐ Phone ☒ Letter
Query first. Responds if interested.

✉ Email: sleepingbearpress@gale.com
🌐 Web Site: http://www.sleepingbearpress.com

SoftPlay, Inc.

3535 W. Peterson Avenue, Chicago, IL 60659
(773) 509 0707

Established:	1986	# of Employees:	–
Titles in Print:	300	Published Annually:	75

What They Publish

Publishes illustrated interactive cloth activity books for children aged six months to three years. Publishes felt play sets for children aged three to five years.

Representative Titles/Projects

- *My First Busy Book*
- *Good Night Elmo*
- *Rescue Heroes Save the Day*

Who They Hire

Writers:
Pays flat fee/pays advances. Holds copyright.

Editors, proofreaders, illustrators, designers, indexers, production personnel:
Rates vary. Send cover letter with current résumé.

Internships/Summer Jobs:
Internships available: ☐ Yes ☒ No   Summer Jobs Available: ☐ Yes ☒ No

How to Get Connected

Contact:
Dan Blau, President

Accepts unsolicited/unagented manuscripts: ☒ Yes ☐ No
Accepts queries by: ☐ Email ☐ Fax ☐ Phone ☒ Letter
Send manuscript with SASE. Do not show up without an appointment. Responds in 8–10 weeks.

✉ Email: dblau@softplayforkids.com
🌐 Web Site: http://softplayforkids.com

Standard Publishing Co.

8121 Hamilton Avenue, Cincinnati, OH 45231
(513) 931 4050

Established:	1866	# of Employees:	300
Titles in Print:	–	Published Annually:	–

What They Publish

Publishes inspirational books for children, tweens, and teens.

Representative Titles/Projects

- *I'd Be Your Princess*
- *Living the Gold-Medal Life*
- Baby Blessings Books

Who They Hire

Authors/Writers:
Pays royalties/advances. Buys all rights.

Editors, proofreaders, illustrators, designers, production personnel:
Rates vary. Send cover letter with current résumé.

Internships/Summer Jobs:
Internships available: ☐ Yes ☒ No   Summer Jobs Available: ☐ Yes ☒ No

How to Get Connected

Contact:
Publisher

Accepts unsolicited/unagented manuscripts: ☒ Yes   ☐ No
Accepts queries by: ☐ Email ☐ Fax ☐ Phone ☒ Letter
Query first. Responds if interested.

✉ Email:
🌐 Web Site: http://www.standardpub.com

Starscape

An Imprint of Tor
175 Fifth Avenue, New York, NY 10010
(212) 388 0100

Established:	–	# of Employees:	–
Titles in Print:	–	Published Annually:	–

What They Publish

Publishes young adult science fiction and fantasy lines.

Representative Titles/Projects

- *Ender's Game*
- *A College of Magics*
- *Red Unicorn*

Who They Hire

Authors/Writers:
Pays royalties/advances. Buys all rights.

Editors, proofreaders, illustrators, designers, production personnel:
Rates vary. Send cover letter with current résumé.

Internships/Summer Jobs:
Internships available: ☒ Yes ☐ No   Summer Jobs Available: ☐ Yes ☒ No

How to Get Connected

Contact:
Jonathan Schmidt, Publisher

Accepts unsolicited/unagented manuscripts: ☐ Yes ☒ No
Accepts queries by: ☐ Email ☐ Fax ☐ Phone ☒ Letter
Query only. Responds if interested.

✉ Email:
🌐 Web Site: http://www.starscapebooks.com

Sunstone Press

PO Box 2321, Santa Fe, NM 87504-2321
(800) 243 5644

Established:	1971	# of Employees:	–
Titles in Print:	–	Published Annually:	–

What They Publish

Publishes novels, Native American, health, cookbooks, regional, and children's books.

Representative Titles/Projects

- *Ace Flies Like an Eagle*
- *Billy the Kid*
- *Yellow Bear Lodge*

Who They Hire

Authors/Writers:
Pays royalties/advances. Buys all rights.

Editors, proofreaders, illustrators, designers, production personnel:
Rates vary. Send cover letter with current résumé.

Internships/Summer Jobs:
Internships available: ☐ Yes ☒ No   Summer Jobs Available: ☐ Yes ☒ No

How to Get Connected

Contact:
James Clois Smith, Jr., Publisher

Accepts unsolicited/unagented manuscripts: ☒ Yes ☐ No
Accepts queries by: ☐ Email ☐ Fax ☐ Phone ☒ Letter
Query first. Responds if interested.

✉ Email: jsmith@sunstonepress.com
🌐 Web Site: http://www.sunstonepress.com

Tanglewood Press

PO Box 3009, Terre Haute, IN 47803
(812) 877 9488

Established:	2002	# of Employees:	–
Titles in Print:	–	Published Annually:	–

What They Publish

Publishes books for small children.

Representative Titles/Projects

- *It All Began With a Bean*
- *Mystery at Blackbeard's Cove*
-

Who They Hire

Authors/Writers:
Pays royalties/advances. Buys all rights.

Editors, proofreaders, illustrators, designers, production personnel:
Rates vary. Send cover letter with current résumé.

Internships/Summer Jobs:
Internships available: ☐ Yes ☒ No   Summer Jobs Available: ☐ Yes ☒ No

How to Get Connected

Contact:
Peggy Tierney, Publisher

Accepts unsolicited/unagented manuscripts: ☒ Yes ☐ No
Accepts queries by: ☐ Email ☐ Fax ☐ Phone ☐ Letter
No queries; complete manuscripts only. Submission guidelines on website.

✉ Email:
🌐 Web Site: http://www.tanglewoodbooks.com

Third World Press

P.O. Box 19730, Chicago, IL 60619
(773) 651 0700

Established:	1967	# of Employees:	6
Titles in Print:	70	Published Annually:	10

What They Publish

Publishes books by and about African Americans; children's fiction and nonfiction; preschool readers, picture books, vocational books; fiction and nonfiction—primarily politics, cultural history, philosophy, and poetry for African American adults and children.

Currently looking for biographical, spiritual, educational, political, and health-related works.

Representative Titles/Projects

- *I Look at Me*
- *The Story of Kwanzaa*
- *The Sweetest Berry on the Bush*

Who They Hire

Writers:
Pays sliding royalty rate seven to ten percent/advances. Retains all rights. Looking for writers with originality in style as well as thoroughness in research and documentation.

Copyeditors, artists, proofreaders, illustrators, designers, indexers, production personnel, and webmasters:
Rates negotiable. Submit current résumé.

Internships/Summer Jobs:
Internships available: ☐ Yes ☒ No   Summer Jobs Available: ☐ Yes ☒ No

How to Get Connected

Contact:
Gwendolyn Mitchell, Editor

Accepts unsolicited/unagented manuscripts: ☒ Yes ☐ No
Accepts queries by: ☐ Email ☐ Fax ☐ Phone ☐ Letter
Accepts unsolicited work in January and July. Responds in 8–10 weeks.

✉ Email: twpress3@aol.com
🌐 Web Site: http://www.thirdworldpressinc.com

Thomas Nelson Children's Division

PO Box 141000, Nashville, TN 37214
(615) 902 3308

Established:	1798	# of Employees:	600
Titles in Print:	–	Published Annually:	–

What They Publish

Publishes children's books.

Representative Titles/Projects

- *Hermie: A Common Caterpillar*
- *He Chase You*
- *I Hope You Dance!*

Who They Hire

Authors/Writers:
Pays royalties/advances. Buys all rights.

Editors, proofreaders, illustrators, designers, production personnel:
Rates vary. Send cover letter with current résumé.

Internships/Summer Jobs:
Internships available: ☐ Yes ☒ No   Summer Jobs Available: ☐ Yes ☒ No

How to Get Connected

Contact:
Editorial Department

Accepts unsolicited/unagented manuscripts: ☐ Yes ☒ No
Accepts queries by: ☐ Email ☐ Fax ☐ Phone ☐ Letter

✉ Email:
🌐 Web Site: http://www.thomasnelson.com

Tiger Tales

An Imprint of ME Media, LLC
202 Old Ridgefield Road, Wilton, CT 06897
(203) 834 0005

Established:	–	# of Employees:	–
Titles in Print:	–	Published Annually:	–

What They Publish

Publishes picture books for children ages 6 months through 8 years of age.

Representative Titles/Projects

- *Animal Actions*
- *Babies Play*
- *Can't You Sleep, Dotty?*

Who They Hire

Authors/Writers:
Pays royalties/advances. Buys all rights.

Editors, proofreaders, illustrators, designers, production personnel:
Rates vary. Send cover letter with current résumé.

Internships/Summer Jobs:
Internships available: ☐ Yes ☒ No   Summer Jobs Available: ☐ Yes ☒ No

How to Get Connected

Contact:
Elisabeth Prial, Publisher

Accepts unsolicited/unagented manuscripts: ☒ Yes ☐ No
Accepts queries by: ☐ Email ☐ Fax ☐ Phone ☒ Letter
Query first. Responds if interested.

✉ Email:
🌐 Web Site: http://www.tigertalesbooks.com

Tilbury House, Publishers

2 Mechanic Street, Gardiner, ME 04345
(207) 582 1899

Established:	1990	# of Employees:	7
Titles in Print:	–	Published Annually:	–

What They Publish

Publishes children's books and teacher's guides about cultural diversity, nature, and the environment.

Representative Titles/Projects

- *Say Something*
- *The Carpet Boy's Gift*
- *The Goat Lady*

Who They Hire

Authors/Writers:
Pays royalties/advances. Buys all rights.

Editors, proofreaders, illustrators, designers, production personnel:
Rates vary. Send cover letter with current résumé.

Internships/Summer Jobs:
Internships available: ☐ Yes ☒ No   Summer Jobs Available: ☐ Yes ☒ No

How to Get Connected

Contact:
Jennifer Bunting, Publisher

Accepts unsolicited/unagented manuscripts: ☒ Yes ☐ No
Accepts queries by: ☐ Email ☐ Fax ☐ Phone ☒ Letter
Submission guidelines on website.

✉ Email:
🌐 Web Site: http://www.www.tilburyhouse.com

Tricycle Press

PO Box 7123, Berkeley, CA 94707
(510) 559 1600

Established:	1993	# of Employees:	–
Titles in Print:	–	Published Annually:	–

What They Publish

Publishes books for children of all ages.

Representative Titles/Projects

- *Pretend Soup*
- Edgar & Ellen Series
- *The Pickle Patch Bathtub*

Who They Hire

Authors/Writers:
Pays royalties/advances. Buys all rights.

Editors, proofreaders, illustrators, designers, production personnel:
Rates vary. Send cover letter with current résumé.

Internships/Summer Jobs:
Internships available: ☐ Yes ☒ No   Summer Jobs Available: ☐ Yes ☒ No

How to Get Connected

Contact:
Nicole Geiger, Publisher
Abigail Samoun, Assistant Editor

Accepts unsolicited/unagented manuscripts: ☐ Yes ☐ No
Accepts queries by: ☐ Email ☐ Fax ☐ Phone ☒ Letter
Submission guidelines on website.

✉ Email:
🌐 Web Site: http://www.tenspeed.com

Tyndale House Publishers

351 Executive Drive, Carol Stream, IL 60188
(630) 668 8300

Established:	1962	# of Employees:	300
Titles in Print:	1300	Published Annually:	120

What They Publish

Publishes a full Bible line, books for the Evangelical Christian adult and children's markets including: home and family, Christian living, fiction, children's picture books, youth fiction and nonfiction, and activity, puzzle, and humor books for adults and children.

Representative Titles/Projects

- Left Behind Series, by Tim LaHaye and Jerry B. Jenkins
- *Let's Roll*, by Lisa Beamer
- *The Last Days of Eugene Meltsner*

Who They Hire

Writers:
Pays royalty rate ten to eighteen percent/pays advances. Rights vary.

Copyeditors, proofreaders, and substantive editors:
Rates negotiable. Submit current résumé.

Internships/Summer Jobs:
Internships available: ☒ Yes ☐ No   Summer Jobs Available: ☐ Yes ☒ No

How to Get Connected

Contact:
Ron Beers, Senior VP, Group Publisher
Cliff Johnson, Douglas Knox, VP, Group Publishers

Accepts unsolicited/unagented manuscripts: ☒ Yes   ☐ No
Accepts queries by: ☐ Email ☐ Fax ☐ Phone ☒ Letter
Write for writer's guidelines. Send query letter with résumé, table of contents, and a detailed synopsis. For fiction, also send sample chapter. Must include an SASE. Do not phone, show up without an appointment, or send complete manuscripts. Responds in 4–12 weeks.

✉ Email: manuscript@tyndale.com
🌐 Web Site: http://www.tyndale.com

The United Educators Inc.

Subsidiary of Standard Education Corporation
900 North Shore Drive, Suite 140, Lake Bluff, IL 60044
(847) 234 3700

Established:	1993	# of Employees:	–
Titles in Print:	–	Published Annually:	–

What They Publish

Publishes encyclopedias and subscription books.

Representative Titles/Projects

- *My Book House*
- *Road to Reading*
- *Universe and Space*

Who They Hire

Writers:
Pays royalties/advances. Buys all rights.

Editors, proofreaders, illustrators, designers, indexers, production personnel:
Rates vary. Send cover letter with current résumé.

Internships/Summer Jobs:
Internships available: ☐ Yes ☒ No   Summer Jobs Available: ☐ Yes ☒ No

How to Get Connected

Contact:
Remo D. Piazzi, President

Accepts unsolicited/unagented manuscripts: ☐ Yes   ☒ No
Accepts queries by: ☐ Email ☐ Fax ☐ Phone ☒ Letter
Do not send unsolicited manuscripts. Prospective authors should send an SASE with their work.
Responds in 2 weeks.

✉ Email:
🌐 Web Site: http://www.theunitededucatorsinc.com

Urban Research Press

840 E 87th Street, Chicago, IL 60619
(773) 994 7200

Established:	1969	# of Employees:	–
Titles in Print:	18	Published Annually:	3

What They Publish

Publishes biographies of well-known African Americans and Jazz musicians; books about real estate, finance and social studies; and children's books.

Representative Titles/Projects

- *Autobiography of Black Jazz*
- *The American Story in Red, White, and Blue*
- *Norman Granz: The White Moses of Black Jazz*

Who They Hire

Writers:
Check directly with publisher for contract information and writer's guidelines.

Copyeditors, proofreaders, designers, and indexers:
Currently not hiring freelance help.

Internships/Summer Jobs:
Internships available: ☐ Yes ☒ No   Summer Jobs Available: ☐ Yes ☒ No

How to Get Connected

Contact:
Dempsey J. Travis, Publisher

Accepts unsolicited/unagented manuscripts: ☐ Yes ☐ No
Accepts queries by: ☐ Email ☐ Fax ☐ Phone ☒ Letter
Do not send complete manuscripts. Responds in 12 weeks.

Email: travisdt88@aol.com
Web Site: http://www.urbanresearchpress.com

Veronica Lane Books

513 Wiltshire Boulevard, Suite 282, Santa Monica, CA 90401
(310) 315 9162

Established:	–	# of Employees:	–
Titles in Print:	–	Published Annually:	–

What They Publish

Publishes the best-selling *What Is?* series on God, death, love, and beauty.

Representative Titles/Projects

- *What Is God?*
- *What Is Funny?*
- *What Is Beautiful?*

Who They Hire

Authors/Writers:
Pays royalties/advances. Buys all rights.

Editors, proofreaders, illustrators, designers, production personnel:
Rates vary. Send cover letter with current résumé.

Internships/Summer Jobs:
Internships available: ☐ Yes ☒ No   Summer Jobs Available: ☐ Yes ☒ No

How to Get Connected

Contact:
Jim Gray, Publisher

Accepts unsolicited/unagented manuscripts: ☐ Yes ☐ No
Accepts queries by: ☐ Email ☐ Fax ☐ Phone ☒ Letter
Query first. Responds if interested.

✉ Email:
🌐 Web Site: http://www.veronicalanebooks.com

Viking Children's Books

An Imprint of Penguin Putnam
375 Hudson Street, New York, NY 10014
(212) 366 2000

Established:	1933	# of Employees:	–
Titles in Print:	–	Published Annually:	60

What They Publish

Publishes innovative books for young readers—from board books for children to sophisticated fiction and nonfiction for teens.

Representative Titles/Projects

- *Pippi Longstocking*
- *The Stinky Cheese Man*
- *Make Way for Ducklings*

Who They Hire

Authors/Writers:

Pays royalties/advances. Buys all rights.

Editors, proofreaders, illustrators, designers, production personnel:

Rates vary. Send cover letter with current résumé.

Internships/Summer Jobs:

Internships available: ☒ Yes ☐ No   Summer Jobs Available: ☐ Yes ☒ No

How to Get Connected

Contact:

Regina Hayes, Publisher

Accepts unsolicited/unagented manuscripts: ☐ Yes   ☒ No
Accepts queries by: ☐ Email ☐ Fax ☐ Phone ☒ Letter
Query only. Responds if interested.

✉ Email:
🌐 Web Site: http://www.penguinputnam.com

Volcano Press

PO Box 270, Volcano, CA 95689
(800) 879 9636

Established:	1973	# of Employees:	–
Titles in Print:	–	Published Annually:	–

What They Publish

Publishes women's health, family violence issues, and multicultural children's books.

Representative Titles/Projects

- *African Animal Tales*
- *Seeing Red*
- *To Tell the Truth*

Who They Hire

Authors/Writers:

Pays royalties/advances. Buys all rights.

Editors, proofreaders, illustrators, designers, production personnel:

Rates vary. Send cover letter with current résumé.

Internships/Summer Jobs:

Internships available: ☐ Yes ☒ No   Summer Jobs Available: ☐ Yes ☒ No

How to Get Connected

Contact:

Ruth Gottstein, Publisher

Accepts unsolicited/unagented manuscripts: ☒ Yes ☐ No
Accepts queries by: ☐ Email ☐ Fax ☐ Phone ☒ Letter
Query first. Responds if interested.

✉ Email: ruth@volcanopress.com
🌐 Web Site: http://www.volcanopress.com

Waldman House Press

An Imprint of TRISTAN Publishing
2300 Louisiana Avenue North, Golden Valley, MN 55427
(763) 545 1383

Established:	1978	# of Employees:	–
Titles in Print:	–	Published Annually:	–

What They Publish

Publishes illustrated seasonal and children's books.

Representative Titles/Projects

- *Tell Me What We Did Today*
-
-

Who They Hire

Authors/Writers:
Pays royalties/advances. Buys all rights.

Editors, proofreaders, illustrators, designers, production personnel:
Rates vary. Send cover letter with current résumé.

Internships/Summer Jobs:
Internships available: ☒ Yes ☐ No   Summer Jobs Available: ☐ Yes ☒ No

How to Get Connected

Contact:
Brett Waldman, Publisher

Accepts unsolicited/unagented manuscripts: ☒ Yes ☐ No
Accepts queries by: ☒ Email ☐ Fax ☐ Phone ☒ Letter

✉ Email: bwaldman@tristanpublishing.com
🌐 Web Site: http://www.tristanpublishing.com

Walker Young Readers

104 Fifth Avenue, New York, NY 10011
(212) 727 8300

Established:	–	# of Employees:	–
Titles in Print:	–	Published Annually:	–

What They Publish

Publishes books for children through teens.

Representative Titles/Projects

- *Things Change*
- *Absolutely Not*
- *Robots Everywhere*

Who They Hire

Authors/Writers:
Pays royalties/advances. Buys all rights.

Editors, proofreaders, illustrators, designers, production personnel:
Rates vary. Send cover letter with current résumé.

Internships/Summer Jobs:
Internships available: ☐ Yes ☒ No   Summer Jobs Available: ☐ Yes ☒ No

How to Get Connected

Contact:
Emily Easton, Timothy Travaglini, Editors

Accepts unsolicited/unagented manuscripts: ☒ Yes ☐ No
Accepts queries by: ☐ Email ☐ Fax ☐ Phone ☒ Letter
Query first. Responds if interested.

✉ Email:
🌐 Web Site: http://www.walkerbooks.com

Watson-Guptill Publications

770 Broadway, New York, NY 10003
(646) 654 5000

Established:	1937	# of Employees:	–
Titles in Print:	–	Published Annually:	–

What They Publish

This company is primarily an art book publisher, but they do publish how-to and illustrated books for children as well.

Representative Titles/Projects

- Christopher Hart: Kids Draw Series
- *Nocolo's Unicorn*
- *The Wedding Dress Mess*

Who They Hire

Authors/Writers:
Pays royalties/advances. Buys all rights.

Editors, proofreaders, illustrators, designers, production personnel:
Rates vary. Send cover letter with current résumé.

Internships/Summer Jobs:
Internships available: ☐ Yes ☒ No   Summer Jobs Available: ☐ Yes ☒ No

How to Get Connected

Contact:
Julie Mazur, Editor, Children's Books

Accepts unsolicited/unagented manuscripts: ☐ Yes ☐ No
Accepts queries by: ☐ Email ☐ Fax ☐ Phone ☒ Letter
Submission guidelines on website. Responds in 8–10 weeks.

✉ Email:
🌐 Web Site: http://www.watsonguptill.com

Albert Whitman and Company

6340 Oakton Street, Morton Grove, IL 60053
(847) 581 0033

Established:	1919	# of Employees:	–
Titles in Print:	250	Published Annually:	30

What They Publish

Publishes fiction, nonfiction, and language arts for children.

Representative Titles/Projects

- *Fox and Fluff*, by Shutta Crum
- *Wanda's Monster*, by Eileen Spinelli
- *Birthday Zoo*, by Deborah Lee Rose

Who They Hire

Writers:
Pays royalty/may pay advances. Retains all rights.

Illustrators:
Pays royalties with advances. Send samples.

Internships/Summer Jobs:
Internships available: ☒ Yes ☐ No   Summer Jobs Available: ☐ Yes ☒ No

How to Get Connected

Contact:
Kathleen Tucker, Editor-in-Chief

Accepts unsolicited/unagented manuscripts: ☒ Yes   ☐ No
Accepts queries by: ☐ Email ☐ Fax ☐ Phone ☒ Letter
Send for writer's guidelines with SASE. Study previous Albert Whitman books before submitting a manuscript. Do not phone. Responds in 12–16 weeks.

✉ Email: n/a
🌐 Web Site: http://www.awhitmanco.com

Workman Publishing Co.

708 Broadway, New York, NY 10003
(212) 254 5900

Established:	–	# of Employees:	–
Titles in Print:	–	Published Annually:	–

What They Publish

Publishes children's, how-to, cookbook, and humor titles.

Representative Titles/Projects

- *1,400 Things for Kids to Be Happy About*
- *Barnyard Dance!*
- *Philadelphia Chickens*

Who They Hire

Authors/Writers:
Pays royalties/advances. Buys all rights.

Editors, proofreaders, illustrators, designers, production personnel:
Rates vary. Send cover letter with current résumé.

Internships/Summer Jobs:
Internships available: ☒ Yes ☐ No   Summer Jobs Available: ☐ Yes ☒ No

How to Get Connected

Contact:
Peter Workman, Publisher
Katie Workman, Associate Publisher

Accepts unsolicited/unagented manuscripts: ☒Yes ☐ No
Accepts queries by: ☐ Email ☐ Fax ☐ Phone ☒ Letter
Submission guidelines on website.

✉ Email:
🌐 Web Site: http://www.workman.com

World Book, Inc.

233 North Michigan Avenue, 20th Floor, Chicago, IL 60601
(312) 729 5800

Established:	1917	# of Employees:	165
Titles in Print:	300	Published Annually:	–

What They Publish

Publishes educational reference material (encyclopedias, dictionaries, atlases, CD-ROMs) for children of all ages.

Representative Titles/Projects

- *America's Presidents*
- *World Book 2002*
- *Make It Work! History*

Who They Hire

Editors, proofreaders, designers, researchers, indexers:
Pays fee/advances.

All work is done by assignment. World Book keeps a file of freelance editors; there is no guarantee when appropriate assignment will match an editor's skills. The publisher is always interested in editors skilled in developing material for the upper elementary or junior high level, especially those who have written textbooks, medical, or science topics.

Submit current résumé.

Internships/Summer Jobs:
Internships available: ☒ Yes ☐ No   Summer Jobs Available: ☐ Yes ☒ No

How to Get Connected

Contact:
Lettie Zinnamon, Human Resources Manager

Send cover letter and résumé. Replies when assignment is available.

✉ Email: Lettie.Zinnamon@worldbook.com
🌐 Web Site: http://www.worldbook.com

ChicagoWriter.com

For and about the business of writing.

Here's some of what you'll find on ChicagoWriter.com each month:

Writers on Writing ● Word Wrangles ● Superior Vocabulary Builders

ChicagoWriter Date Book ● Write Education

Clients in Focus ● Webliography ● Word Games

News & Trends ● Awards & Contests

Job Links ● Salary Wizard ● Worth Reading

eBooks ● freeBooks ● Communiqués

We're the e-resource for Chicago's
writers, editors, and publishing professionals.

Chicago Writer **Books**
Quick Order Form

Name: _____

Address: _____

City: _____ State: _____ ZIP: _____

Telephone: _____

Email Address: _____

Please send the following books:

# Copies	Title	Price Each	Total
	A Guide to Chicago Book Publishers (ISBN 0-9710878-0-6)	$34.95	
	A Guide to Chicagoland Magazines (ISBN 0-9710878-2-2)	$44.95	
	A Guide to Writing Jobs in Chicago (ISBN 0-9710878-4-9)	$19.95	
	A Guide to Chicago's Multicultural Publishers (ISBN 0-9710878-6-5)	$34.95	
	A Guide to Children's Book Publishers (ISBN 0-9710878-8-1)	$34.95	
	The Write Education (ISBN 1-933048-00-X)	$19.95	
	Please add 6.5% sales tax for all orders shipped to Illinois addresses.	Sales Tax	
	Standard shipping is free. To upgrade to USPS Priority Mail, add $4.00 for the first book and $1.00 for each additional book.	Shipping	
	TOTAL DUE		

Prices listed include free standard shipping to one location.
All orders must be prepaid. Please remit order request along with check or money order in $US to:

iWrite Publications Inc.
PO Box 10923
Chicago, IL 60610-0923

For pricing on our books in ebook format and more information on all of our publications, please visit our website at www.ChicagoWriter.com.